PSALMS

90 DEVOTIONS FROM
OUR DAILY BREAD

COMPILED BY DAVE BRANON

Discovery House.
from Our Daily Bread Ministries

Previously published as *Songs of a Seeking Heart: 90 Devotions on Psalms from Our Daily Bread.*

Discovery House is affiliated with Our Daily Bread Ministries, Grand Rapids, Michigan.

Requests for permission to quote from this book should be directed to: Permissions Department, Discovery House, P.O. Box 3566, Grand Rapids, MI 49501, or contact us by e-mail at permissionsdept@dhp.org.

ISBN: 978-1-62707-488-9

Printed in the United States of America
First printing in 2016

CONTENTS

Foreword	5	Why Worship?	32
		No Thanks	33
The Best Teacher	7	Our Best Defense	34
Igor and Me	8	Cover-ups Stink	36
What's in a Smile?	9	Let's Sing!	37
Early Defense System	10	The Last Jellybean	38
God, Answer Me	12	Just You and God	39
Like a (Huge) Diamond in the Sky	13	The Last Word	40
"I Sure Found Out!"	14	Joy in the Morning	42
God Is Watching	15	"It Never Touched My Heart"	43
Praise for Pressure	16	Really Thirsty	44
It Looks Bad	18	God's Wheelchair	45
Postcard Christianity	19	Plenty to Praise	46
The Best Question	20	Weak Beneath the Surface	48
Sleepless Nights	21	The Voice of God at Sunset	49
Fair-Weather Warning	22	The Wonder of Grace	50
When the Ground Shakes	24	A Fool's Argument	51
Message from the Skies	25	Give Him Your Burden	52
Forsaken	26	When Fear Creeps In	54
Source of Hope	27	Snapping, Snarling Thoughts	55
Valley of the Shadow	28	Filling Up Empty	56
Always with You	30	Eat Fast, Pay Less	57
Regular Checkups	31		

Squirrel Feeder	58
Worship by Prayer	60
Pigs Don't Pray	61
The Other Eighty Percent	62
When Life Seems Unfair	63
Like a Flock	64
Tell the Children	66
Do You Live in a Box?	67
Bull's-Eye	68
Where Are We Going So Fast?	69
Holding On for Life	70
Fresh Fruit	72
Mightier Than All	73
Sustained in the Silence	74
The True Owner	75
Sing Again	76
Just Because He's Good	78
Integrity 101	79
Five-Minute Rule	80
God's Helpers	81
The Universe Is God's	82
Rescue and Response	84
How to Answer Accusers	85
He Lights the Way	86
I Love You, Daddy	87

In Brief	88
A Bad Day?	90
Follow the Signal	91
From Heart to Heart	92
"I Dare You!"	93
The Forgotten Book	94
The Cheat Test	96
A Fair Trade	97
Beyond the Shadows	98
He Never Sleeps	99
Dying in the Service	100
Keep Laughing	102
We All Need Mercy	103
Rained Out!	104
A Safe Pair of Hands	105
Those Inner Flaws	106
Communion on the Moon	108
Wonderfully Made	109
A Fresh Glimpse of Glory	110
Not Enough Stars	111
Hallelujah!	112
A Lesson in Praise	114
Our Daily Bread Writers	115
Note to the Reader	120

FOREWORD

You might remember the *Where's Waldo?* books from the 1980s. They were popular children's picture books about a little guy named Waldo in a hat, glasses, and red-and-white-striped shirt. He hid in the pages among hundreds of other images that made it nearly impossible to find him. The challenge, which was fun yet frustrating for many children and their parents, was to find him on each page.

We have been created to search for Someone who can't even be seen—God. The apostle Paul said that God made people "so that they would seek him and perhaps reach out for him and find him" (Acts 17:27). That sounds so challenging that we might wonder if we could ever actually find Him. But the good news is that God is not at all hard to find, for "he is not far from any one of us" (v. 27). He desires to be known and to make himself known to us. We can find Him on every page of His Word. These verses from the Bible tell us that He can be found:

Seek the LORD while he may be found,
call on him while he is near (Isaiah 55:6).

You will seek me and find me
when you seek me with all your heart (Jeremiah 29:13).

The LORD is good to those whose hope is in him,
to the one who seeks him (Lamentations 3:25).

The *Our Daily Bread* devotional articles and Scripture verses in this book are meant to help you in your personal search for God as you make your way through the book of Psalms. The articles were chosen to help you find Him. The psalmists who sought Him found that He is gracious, perfect, compassionate, holy, and wise. He is high above us all, yet He wants us to know Him personally because we need Him. Take a few moments in these pages to draw near to God, and He will draw near to you.

Your face, LORD, I will seek.

—Anne Cetas, senior editor, Our Daily Bread

THE BEST TEACHER

Read: Psalm 1

Blessed is the one who does not walk in step with the wicked.
—PSALM 1:1

In talking to young people about preparing for the future, I've had several say something like this: "We must get into the world to experience ungodly situations and ungodly people in order to grow stronger."

This kind of thinking has swallowed up many immature Christians and eventually turned them against God. Sure, we're in the world (John 17:15) and we're exposed to non-Christian situations (school, job, neighborhood), but we need to be careful that exposure to those situations does not lead us to embrace ungodly philosophies. All of us would mature faster by following the divine pattern suggested in Psalm 1:1.

First, let's not let our decisions and choices be controlled by the "counsel of the ungodly." Second, we shouldn't put ourselves in a place where those who don't know Jesus can unduly influence our thought processes. Third, let's avoid getting comfortable with those who mock God, His Word, and His role in our life so that their thinking seems right to us.

Trusting the counsel from such sources leads us away from God. Instead, it's best to get our training, our guidance, and our advice from God's holy Word and from people who know it and love it. God and His Word, not experiences, are our best teachers.

—*Dave Branon*

———

The word *blessed* is sometimes rendered *happy*. We see it translated this way in 1 Kings 10:8 and 2 Chronicles 9:7.

IGOR AND ME

Read: Psalm 3

But you, LORD, are a shield around me, my glory, the One who lifts my head high. —PSALM 3:3

When I was visiting Siberia to teach some Bible classes, my friend Igor and I stopped at a store. Just outside the door a large, mean-looking dog snarled at us and would not let us inside. After a while the storeowner came out, and to my surprise he shot the dog. So Igor and I went in.

A few minutes later, four angry Russians burst into the building, looking for the man who had killed their dog. One slapped Igor in the face, and another slammed me against a wall. When they saw that neither of us had a rifle, they left. But they returned almost immediately. After more heated conversation, they left again. Only then did I realize that Igor had positioned himself between me and the half-drunken men. They would have had to fight Igor to get to me—and he is one strong man!

What Igor did for me illustrates what God does for His people. King David's foes were aligned against him, led by his son Absalom. Yet David saw God as his shield (Psalm 3:3). This truth reflected David's own relationship to his people. They saw the king as their shield, their protector against the enemy. Now the king saw the Almighty as his protector.

Whoever may rise up against us—man or spiritual foe—will find our God between us and him. We can trust the Lord to shield us from our foes.

—*David Egner*

———

David wrote this psalm while fleeing from his son Absalom. Just when David may have felt abandoned (vv. 1–2), he recognized that the Lord was his shield, glory, and restorer of dignity.

WHAT'S IN A SMILE?

Read: Psalm 4

Fill my heart with joy. —PSALM 4:7

According to an article in the *New York Times,* the act of smiling can promote good feelings. Writer Daniel Goleman cited experiments in which researchers found that saying the word *cheese* caused a person to smile, which in turn created pleasant feelings. On the other hand, saying the word *few* created a different facial expression, which resulted in negative emotions.

Interesting as such a study may be, there's a better way to have peace and gladness. It works from the inside out, not from the outside in.

In Psalm 4, David set forth several courses of action he took when he was feeling deeply distressed. He asked God for relief and mercy (v. 1). He took comfort in knowing that he was favored by God and that the Lord heard him when he called (v. 3). David was quiet before God (v. 4). He did what was right and put his trust in Him (v. 5). He rested in the assurance of God's peace and safety (v. 8). David was confident that he would receive joy in his heart (v. 7) as a gift from God, not as the result of some forced smile that might bring a temporary good feeling.

Father, help us in our low moments to look up to you. Grant us the peace and gladness that David experienced when he called on you.

—*Mart DeHaan*

The joy of verse 7 is the real deal—and it is directly from God, as contrasted to the temporary gladness of happy circumstances, as the second part of verse 7 addresses.

EARLY DEFENSE SYSTEM

Read: Psalm 5

In the morning, LORD, you hear my voice; in the morning I lay my requests before you. —PSALM 5:3

Every believer in Christ is involved in spiritual warfare every day. We cannot afford, therefore, to enter the day complacently.

In an article for the *San Francisco Chronicle*, Herb Caen wrote, "Every morning in Africa, a gazelle wakes up. It knows it must run faster than the fastest lion or it will be killed. Every morning a lion wakes up. It knows it must outrun the slowest gazelle or it will starve to death. It doesn't matter whether you're a lion or a gazelle; when the sun comes up, you'd better be running."

British pastor Charles Spurgeon wrote, "If you are not seeking the Lord, the devil is seeking you." We must not wait until we are attacked by Satan to think about the strategy we should use to escape the enemy of our soul. We must seek the Lord early, keenly aware that "the devil prowls around like a roaring lion, looking for someone to devour" (1 Peter 5:8).

In Psalm 5 we read that David expressed his need for God's help. He came to the Lord early in the morning, seeking His guidance and protection (vv. 3, 8, 12).

Let's not move into any new day without being aware of our urgent need for the Lord. Being prepared is the best way to be ready for Satan's attack.

—*David Egner*

David's words in Psalm 5 suggest confidence that God is listening: "You hear my voice." This was definitely a prayer of faith.

✕

GOD, ANSWER ME

Read: Psalm 6

Away from me, all you who do evil, for the LORD has heard my weeping.
—PSALM 6:8

Theresa left Sue a message that she had some great news. Sue was convinced that her friend had received Jesus as Savior. After all, she had been praying for Theresa's salvation for 30 years. What could be greater news!

A few days later, Theresa revealed her "great news": She had a new boyfriend and was moving in with him. Sue cried out in desperation, "Lord, what makes me think that You would answer me after 30 years of praying?" She proceeded to have a pity party for herself about God's seeming reluctance to answer her.

Some of our hardest struggles are those deep desires that go unmet—when no response comes from heaven for what seems like forever. The psalmist David could relate. He cried, "Have mercy on me, LORD . . . . My soul is in deep anguish. How long, LORD, how long? Turn, LORD, and deliver me" (Psalm 6:2–4). But later in the psalm we read that David knew the Lord had heard him (v. 9).

A month after Theresa's "great news," she called and left another message: "I have wonderful news! I trusted Jesus as my Savior! I don't know why I didn't do it long ago." Now Sue is praying that Theresa will grow in the Lord and seek to please Him with her life.

Keep praying. In His time, God will answer.

—Anne Cetas

———

The psalmist voices a triumphant message. He confidently casts aside those "who do evil" because of God's intervention.

LIKE A (HUGE) DIAMOND IN THE SKY

Read: Psalm 8

You have made them a little lower than the angels and crowned them with glory and honor. —PSALM 8:5

Astronomers discovered a star in the sky that has cooled and compressed into a giant diamond. The largest rough gem-quality diamond ever found on Earth is the Cullinan Diamond—at over 3,100 carats. So how many carats are in the cosmic diamond? Ten billion trillion trillion carats!

In our world, diamonds are prized for their rarity, beauty, and durability, and we often hear it said, "Diamonds are forever." But God isn't enamored with diamonds. To Him there is something far more precious.

Thousands of years ago, David marveled at the great value God had set on human beings: "What is mankind that you are mindful of them, human beings that you care for them? You have made them a little lower than the angels and crowned them with glory and honor" (Psalm 8:4–5).

In fact, God placed such a high value on us that it cost Him dearly to buy our redemption. The purchase price was the precious blood of His Son, Jesus Christ (1 Peter 1:18–19).

If God places such a high value on us, we should also place a high value on the people He has brought into our lives. Bring them before the Lord in prayer. Ask Him to show you how each is more priceless than the most costly jewel in the universe.

—Dennis Fisher

Bible scholar Geoffrey W. Grogan says about Psalm 8:5, "Nowhere is human dignity more strongly affirmed than here."

"I SURE FOUND OUT!"

Read: Psalm 9

You have rebuked the nations and destroyed the wicked . . . .
The LORD is a refuge for the oppressed, a stronghold in times of trouble.
—PSALM 9:5, 9

Bystanders spotted the nine-year-old boy in the swollen river. He was struggling will all his might to stay afloat in the raging torrent. He did not have the strength to swim to shore, though it was only ten yards away. Rescuers jumped in and pulled him to safety. The boy, exhausted and bedraggled, lay panting on the riverbank. After he caught his breath, someone asked, "Did you fall in?" "No," he said. "I just wanted to see how strong the current was. I sure found out!"

Psalm 9 talks about the strength of the all-powerful God, the Creator, Ruler, and Judge of the universe. It describes what happens to those who decide to challenge His strength or exalt themselves above Him. They soon find out how powerful He really is. They lose their thrones. Their kingdoms crumble. Their armies collapse. Yet the Lord endures forever.

The psalmist gives another side to this all-powerful God, however. He portrays Him as the One who protects and cares for those who take refuge in Him. The same God whose power destroys evil preserves what is good. And no one can break through His protection without His permission.

What a comfort it is to know that God's power can thwart the wicked and protect the righteous! I sure can trust a God like that.

—*David Egner*

What a contrast this psalm provides! The ungodly risk destruction, but God provides hope and help for the oppressed and needy in times of trouble.

GOD IS WATCHING

Read: Psalm 10

But you, God, see the trouble of the afflicted; you consider their grief and take it in hand. —PSALM 10:14

As I scanned the newspaper, I noticed that it carried its usual daily share of bad news: Financial woes. Foreign policy concerns. Domestic squabbles. Nothing out of the ordinary.

Then I turned the page and looked into the beautiful face of a smiling teenager. But she will never smile again on earth. An honor student home from college for the weekend, she decided to go jogging with her dog. The dog came home. She never did. Searchers found her body several days later. Murdered.

The story stopped me cold. Not again, I thought. Not another innocent victim. Not another family left to grieve the senseless loss of a precious daughter. Not more dashed hopes and shattered dreams. Why do the young keep dying at the hands of ruthless killers?

I found the answer in Psalm 10. The wicked person does what he does because "in all his thoughts there is no room for God" (v. 4). "From ambush he murders the innocent" (v. 8), thinking, "God will never notice" (v. 11). Murder and violence result when people don't think God notices what they do. But God sees, and He will avenge the murder of the innocent (vv. 14–15).

Yes, God is still on the throne. Evil men may think they're getting away with murder, but we can be assured that God's justice will prevail.

—*Dave Branon*

———

How comforting it is to know that God is on the lookout for trouble and, when He finds it, helps us by dealing with it.

PRAISE FOR PRESSURE

Read: Psalm 11

The LORD examines the righteous, but the wicked, those who love violence,
he hates with a passion. —PSALM 11:5

A young man was fascinated by a moth and performed a little experiment to see what would happen when it was released from its cocoon without a struggle. Using his pocketknife, he slit the enclosure, allowing the insect to emerge freely. However, it had none of the expected color, it couldn't fly, and it soon died. As he thought about this, he concluded that the pressure exerted on an emerging moth is essential to its proper development—yes, to its very existence! He later learned that through the moth's struggle to free itself, its body fluids are stimulated and the luster is developed on its wings. So too for the Christian, life's pressures can produce positive results.

A dear saint of God, almost a century old, said, "As I look back over my long life, the dealings of God that were bitterest at the time are now sweetest as I remember them and understand His purposes." The songwriter put it like this: "When fierce temptations try my heart, I'll sing, 'Jesus is mine!' And so, though tears at times may start, I'm singing all the time." Most of us must confess we find it difficult to sing in times of sorrow, suffering, and trial. Yet, if we understood that God has a reason for either ordering or allowing every pressure we face, rejoicing would more readily flow from our hearts.

Bitter disappointments, painful suffering, and shattering sorrow, if accepted in faith, can be a means of strengthening our character. What peace is ours when we learn to praise Him for the pressure!

—*Paul Van Gorder*

Psalm 11 uses strong language
to describe those who perpetrate evil.
But the language is fitting,
for God hates evil.

IT LOOKS BAD

Read: Psalm 12

"Because the poor are plundered and the needy groan, I will now arise,"
says the Lord. —PSALM 12:5

King David looked out at the world and was troubled. He didn't need the Internet to paint a bleak picture of society or the *New York Times* to remind him of crime and suffering. Even without a cable news show to give him all the bad news, he saw the evil.

He looked around and saw that "those who are loyal have vanished" and that "no one is faithful anymore." In his world, everyone lied to their neighbors and "flatter[ed] with their lips but harbor[ed] deception in their hearts" (Psalm 12:1–2).

This description may sound like the theme of a TV show, but it was life circa 1,000 BC. While we may view society's evils as much worse than anything before, David reminds us that evil is not a twenty-first-century innovation.

But David's words also give us hope. Notice his reaction to the bad news he bore. In verse 1, he turned to God and cried, "Help!" Then he implored God with specific needs. The response he got was positive. God promised that because He rules righteously, He would provide protection and safety (vv. 5–7).

When you are discouraged by all the bad news, cry out for God's help. Then bask in the confidence of His assurance. Three thousand years after David, God is still, and always will be, in control.

—*Dave Branon*

God's verbal response in this song is the first such direct answer in the Psalms. It reassures the reader that God cares for those in need and clearly stands ready to assist!

POSTCARD CHRISTIANITY

Read: Psalm 13

*How long, LORD? Will you forget me forever? How long
will you hide your face from me?* —PSALM 13:1

When my husband and I visited Mount Rainier, one of the highest points in the continental United States, I expected to see some spectacular sights. But for two days the mountain remained shrouded in clouds. So instead of taking pictures, I bought postcards.

Our vacation caused me to question the way I portray my faith to people around me. Do I present a "postcard" view of Christianity? Do I give the false impression that my life is always sunny—that my view of God is always clear?

That's not what David did. In the passion-filled poetry of Psalm 13, he admitted that he couldn't see God and didn't understand what He was doing (v. 1). But by the end of his prayer, he was certain that what he couldn't see was nevertheless there because he had seen it before in God's bountiful care (vv. 5–6).

Christians are like people living at the foot of Mount Rainier. They've seen the mountain before, so they know it exists even when clouds are covering it.

When suffering or confusion obscures our view of God, we can be honest with others about our doubts. But we can also express our confidence that the Lord is still there by recalling times we've witnessed His grandeur and goodness. That's better than postcard Christianity.

—*Julie Ackerman Link*

The psalmist seems to feel like a neglected friend, and it hurts. He longs to see the face of God—to experience a close relationship once again. By the end of Psalm 13, his relationship with God has been reestablished.

THE BEST QUESTION

Read: Psalm 15:1

*LORD, who may dwell in your sacred tent? Who may live
on your holy mountain?* —PSALM 15:1

Nobel Prize–winning physicist Martin Perl was asked what he attributed his success to. "My mother," he answered. "Every day when I came home from school, she asked me, 'So, Marty, did you ask any good questions today?' "

David asked the best question of all: "LORD, who may dwell in your sacred tent?" (Psalm 15:1). There are two words ancient Jews had for expressing the question "who?" One is similar to our usage. But David used another word here that asks, "What kind of person dwells close to God?"

The answer came in a series of character traits: "The one whose walk is blameless, who does what is righteous, who speaks the truth from their heart" (v. 2).

It's one thing to know the truth; it's another to obey it. God delights to live on His holy mountain with those who are holy—who reflect the reality of the truth they believe. He loves men and women who "ring true."

This psalm, however, is not about any holiness of our own that we think will qualify us to gain entrance to His presence. It is rather about the beauty of holiness that God forms in us as we dwell in fellowship with Him.

The closer we get to God, the more like Him we will become.
—*David McCasland*

___

This psalm asks: Who can dwell in a close relationship with God? Today, because of Jesus's death and resurrection, all who believe in Him are made holy and are in a close relationship with Him!

SLEEPLESS NIGHTS

Read: Psalm 16

I will praise the LORD, who counsels me; even at night my heart instructs me. —PSALM 16:7

The psalmist David had his dark, lonely nights when everything seemed out of control. Doubts and fears assailed him, and there was no escape from his problems. He tossed and turned just as we do, but then he turned to his Shepherd (Psalm 23:1) and reminded himself of the Lord's presence. That brought peace to his anxious, troubled soul. David said, "With him at my right hand, I will not be shaken" (16:8).

We too have occasions of wakefulness when anxious thoughts jostle one another for attention, when we curse the darkness, and when we long for sleep. But we mustn't fret, for darkness can be our friend. God is present in it, visiting us, counseling us, instructing us in the night. Perhaps on our beds, as nowhere else, we may hear God's voice. We can listen to His thoughts and meditate on His Word.

We can talk to the Lord about every concern, casting our care on Him (1 Peter 5:7). We can talk about our failures, our conflicts, our challenges, our anxieties, our frustrations over His lengthy delays—all the things that stress us out and render us sleepless—and listen to what He has to say. That's what can set us apart from ordinary insomniacs. That's the secret of quiet rest.

—Haddon Robinson

The literal meaning of the word translated as *heart* in verse 7 is *kidneys*, considered the innermost place of emotions and thought. Other translations use *mind*, *conscience*, or *reins*.

FAIR-WEATHER WARNING

Read: Psalm 16

The boundary lines have fallen for me in pleasant places;
surely I have a delightful inheritance. —PSALM 16:6

Adversity can pose real dangers to the Christian. Doubt, discouragement, and depression lurk in the dim shadows of hard times, making us especially vulnerable to temptation and sin. Periods of relative calm, however, can be equally treacherous. Feelings of self-sufficiency can cause us to let down our guard—and that can spell trouble.

Adventurer Harry Pidgeon, who circled the globe in a small sailboat, was asked to relate some of his experiences. He said, "Do you know the most dangerous thing a man sailing alone has to face?" "I suppose storms and rocks," responded the interviewer. "You're wrong," said Pidgeon. "It wasn't storms I was afraid of; but the clear, calm weather when a good breeze was blowing. In a gale when a man goes on deck, he holds fast to something, for he knows he might fall overboard, but in fair weather he's apt to walk around the deck without thinking. Then a little roll of the boat can throw him overboard and he is lost."

We're not sure of David's circumstances when he wrote Psalm 16, but his heart attitude was centered on the Lord so that no matter what the "weather," he would remain secure. He affirmed his trust in God (v. 1), acknowledged Him as his highest treasure (v. 2), and determined to keep Him uppermost in his thoughts (v. 8).

If you are in a period of life that's free from sickness, financial stress, and other adverse pressures, thank God. But, like David, stay alert! A fair-weather warning is always out when life's waters are calm.

—*Dennis DeHaan*

Psalm 16:6 holds a certain enthusiasm and exuberance. Why? Because David is celebrating his inheritance— his true riches as an heir of God.

)X(

WHEN THE GROUND SHAKES

Read: Psalm 18

In my distress I called to the LORD; I cried to my God for help.
From his temple he heard my voice. —PSALM 18:6

Several days after a devastating earthquake in the San Francisco area, a young boy was seen rocking and swaying on the school playground. His principal asked him if he was okay, and the boy nodded yes and said, "I am moving like the earth, so if there's another earthquake I won't feel it." He wanted to prepare himself for another shaking of the ground.

Sometimes after a trauma, we brace ourselves for what might be coming next. If we've had a phone call that brought bad news, every time the phone rings we feel panicky and wonder, *What has happened now?*

The "ground was shaking" for the psalmist David after King Saul tried to kill him (1 Samuel 19:10). He ran and hid. He thought death was next and told his friend Jonathan, "There is only a step between me and death" (20:3). He wrote, "The cords of death entangled me; the torrents of destruction overwhelmed me" (Psalm 18:4).

David cried to the Lord in his distress (v. 6) and found that He was a stabilizer, One he could trust would always be with him. He said, "The LORD is my rock, my fortress and my deliverer; my God is my rock, in whom I take refuge, . . . my stronghold" (v. 2). The Lord will be that for us also when the ground shakes under us.

—*Anne Cetas*

Notice the metaphors David uses to describe his troubles: "The cords of death entangled me" (v. 4) and the "torrents of destruction overwhelmed me" (v. 4). Ever been there?

MESSAGE FROM THE SKIES

Read: Psalm 19

The heavens declare the glory of God; the skies proclaim the work of his hands. —PSALM 19:1

The earth's population is now over seven billion. And depending on where we live, finding moments of solitude where we can gaze at the silent night sky is increasingly difficult. Yet, according to the writer of Psalm 19, if we were able to steal away to a spot where the only sound was our heartbeat and the only sight the canopy of the stars, we could hear a message from those heavens.

In such a moment, we could hear with the ears of our innermost being the noiseless testimony of God's breathtaking creation.

We could hear from the heavens as they "declare the glory of God" (v. 1). And we could watch in amazement as the "skies proclaim the work of his hands" (v. 1).

We could listen as "day after day they pour forth speech" that fills our minds with the unmistakable awareness of God's splendid creation (v. 2).

We could marvel through the night as the firmament shows in unmistakable splendor the knowledge of God's handiwork (vv. 1–2).

Our Creator tells us to "be still, and know that I am God" (Psalm 46:10). A great way to do this is to spend time in His creation admiring His handiwork. Then we will certainly know that He is God!

—*Dave Branon*

———

Bible scholar H. C. Leupold describes the majesty of verse 1 in this way: "It is as if the word *glory* were written in capital letters across the very heavens."

FORSAKEN

Read: Psalm 22

The poor will eat and be satisfied; those who seek the LORD will praise him. —PSALM 22:26

Do you know which psalm is quoted most often in the New Testament? You may have guessed the familiar and beloved twenty-third Psalm, but actually it is Psalm 22. This psalm begins with David's poignant, heart-breaking words that were quoted by Jesus on the cross, "My God, my God, why have you forsaken me?" (Matthew 27:46; Mark 15:34).

Imagine the situation David must have found himself in that caused him to cry out to God in this way. Notice that he felt forsaken and abandoned: "Why are you so far from saving me?" (Psalm 22:1). He also felt ignored: "My God, I cry out by day, but you do not answer" (v. 2).

Ever been there? Have you ever looked up into the heavens and wondered why it seemed that God had abandoned you, or was ignoring you? Welcome to David's world. But for every plaintive cry David expresses, there is a characteristic of God mentioned that rescues him from despondency. Through it all, David discovers that God is holy (v. 3), trustworthy (vv. 4–5), a deliverer and rescuer (vv. 8, 20–21), and strong (v. 19).

Do you feel forsaken? Seek the Lord. Rehearse His character. And "let your heart rejoice with everlasting joy" (v. 26 NLT).

—*Dave Branon*

———

The language of Psalm 22:26 mirrors that of the feast of the peace offering of Leviticus 7. At that feast, poor friends would be invited to share in the joy.

SOURCE OF HOPE

Read: Psalm 23

You have been my hope, Sovereign LORD, my confidence since my youth.
—PSALM 71:5

The ancient road from Jerusalem to Jericho is a narrow, treacherous path along a deep gorge in the Judean wilderness. Its name is Wadi Kelt, but it's known as the valley of the shadow, for this is the location that inspired David's Psalm 23. The place itself offers little reason to compose such a hopeful poem. The landscape is bleak, barren, and perilously steep. It's a good place for thieves, but not for anyone else.

When David wrote, "Even though I walk through the darkest valley, I will fear no evil" (v. 4), he was in a place where evil was an ever-present reality. Yet he refused to give in to fear. He wasn't expressing hope that God would abolish evil so that he could pass through safely; he was saying that the presence of God gave him the confidence to pass through difficult places without fear of being deserted by Him. In another psalm, David said that the Lord was his hope (71:5).

Many claim to have hope, but only those whose hope is Christ can claim it with certainty. Hope comes not from strength, intelligence, or favorable circumstances, but from the Lord. As Maker of heaven and earth, He alone has the right to promise hope and the power to keep that promise.

—*Julie Ackerman Link*

Think about these words of author David Roper: "When we come to the end of all valleys, we'll understand that every path has been selected, out of all possible options, for our ultimate good."

VALLEY OF THE SHADOW

Read: Psalm 23

Even though I walk through the darkest valley, I will fear no evil, for you are with me. —PSALM 23:4

Darkness upon darkness. Sorrow upon sorrow. Pain upon pain. Anguish upon anguish. That's death.

Death is a fearful visitor, snatching away people who are precious to us and leaving us behind to mourn, grieve, and wonder. It blocks the light that before had shined so freely and easily on our lives.

Whether we're facing the prospect of dying, or dealing with the death of a loved one, death can be devastating. It can sap our energy, change our plans, overwhelm our soul, alter our outlook, test our faith, steal our joy, and challenge our assumptions about life's purposes.

When we walk through the deep valley, we feel swallowed up by the shadow and come face-to-face with fear. The frantic emptiness of our loss threatens the comfort that previously originated from our trust in God, and so we grow afraid. Afraid of our future. Afraid to enjoy life again.

Yet in that valley, under that shadow, we can say to the Lord, "I will fear no evil, for you are with me" (Psalm 23:4). His loving arms never let us go. He is always with us.

Slowly at first, but most assuredly, He provides comfort and release from the darkness. He gives light. He leads us out. Eventually, we escape the valley of the shadow.

—*Dave Branon*

At the point of greatest need—
in the valley of the shadow of death—
the Lord is beside us, comforting
and protecting us. He is an escort
through life's worst days.

ALWAYS WITH YOU

Read: Psalm 25:4-10

I am with you and will watch over you wherever you go.
—GENESIS 28:15

The highway that winds around the southern shore of Lake Michigan can be treacherous in the winter. One weekend as we were driving back to Grand Rapids from Chicago, a buildup of snow and ice slowed traffic, caused numerous accidents, and almost doubled our drive time. We were relieved as we eased off the expressway onto our final road. It was then that my husband said out loud, "Thanks, Lord. I think I can take it from here."

Just as he finished saying the words, our car spun around 180 degrees. As we came to a stop, hearts pounding, we could just imagine God saying: "Are you sure?"

Why do we sometimes try to go it alone in life when at every moment we have access to God? He said, "I am with you and will watch over you wherever you go" (Genesis 28:15). And He assures us: "Never will I leave you; never will I forsake you" (Hebrews 13:5).

Scottish mathematician, theologian, and preacher Thomas Chalmers (1780–1847) wrote, "When I walk by the wayside, He is along with me. When I enter into company, amid all my forgetfulness of Him, He never forgets me. . . . Go where I will, He tends me, and watches me, and cares for me."

What a comfort to know that God is always with us—we don't need to go through life alone!

—*Cindy Hess Kasper*

Even in the midst of asking for God's "ways" and "truth" and "great mercy and love" (vv. 4-6), the psalmist also acknowledges his sin before God. God is our refuge in spite of our failures.

REGULAR CHECKUPS

Read: Psalm 26

Test me, LORD, and try me. —PSALM 26:2

While visiting a neighborhood store, a teenager by the name of Jimmy made a phone call that was overheard by the store-owner.

The conversation went something like this: "Hello. Is this Mr. Brown? I was wondering whether you needed anyone to cut your grass. Oh, you already have someone? Is he doing a good job? He is? Are you sure you don't want to hire someone else? You're positive? All right, then. Thank you. Goodbye."

As the boy hung up, the owner of the store approached the teen and said, "I'm sorry, Jimmy, that you didn't get that job." "Oh, don't worry about that," answered Jimmy. "I already work for Mr. Brown. I was just checking up on myself."

As believers in Christ, we too should check up on ourselves regularly. Because we desire to be approved by our Lord, we should invite Him to examine every area of our lives—our relationship with other Christians, our obedience to the Word of God, and our testimony for Him. If the result of this heart-searching reveals any shortcomings, we should correct them. Doing this on a regular basis will help prevent the consequences of God's disapproval.

Is it time for a checkup?

—*Richard DeHaan*

———

While Psalm 26 can serve as a checklist of integrity for us, for David it was a psalm of vindication in which he responds to those who have maligned him.

WHY WORSHIP?

Read: Psalm 27

Wait for the LORD; be strong and take heart and wait for the LORD.
—PSALM 27:14

Why bother going to church? Some would tell us that it's better to sleep late on Sunday, eat a leisurely breakfast, and lounge around talking with the family. And then maybe have lunch with friends or enjoy a picnic and games with the children. "Make it a day that's different and even restful," some would say, "but don't waste time by going to church on Sunday!"

Worship? Who needs worship anyway?

We all do! We need worship because we are unique creatures made in the image of God. We are made for God, so we can't fulfill our purpose unless we develop a right relationship with Him. And worship helps us to do that when we focus on the Lord.

As we join with other worshipers in church, our hearts are lifted out of this temporal world into God's eternal world. According to British clergyman William Temple, in worship the *conscience* is quickened by the holiness of God, the *mind* is fed by the truth of God, the *imagination* is purged by the beauty of God, the *heart* is opened to the love of God, and the *will* is devoted to the purpose of God. And thus we are helped onward in our goal of becoming more like God.

Let's decide now that on Sunday we will be in church with a heart prepared to worship.

—*Vernon Grounds*

David's reference to the tabernacle, or "sacred tent" (27:5), may have been symbolic here—speaking of the sanctuary of God's presence. And as verse 14 indicates, His presence is worth waiting for.

NO THANKS

Read: Psalm 28

LORD my God, I will praise you forever. —PSALM 30:12

While I was teaching at a Christian college, a talented young man pushed his way into my life. He needed one more course to graduate, so he decided that I should give him an independent study in writing. He would be everlastingly grateful if I would just do this—even though it required extra work on my part. The college dean agreed to the idea because of the young man's abilities.

What a headache! He skipped appointments, missed deadlines, and rejected my evaluations of his writing. He turned in the last assignment just hours before graduation.

After all that was done for him, you'd think he would have been grateful. But he didn't express one word of thanks on graduation day or in all the years since.

I don't ever want to be that kind of person. I would rather be like David. When he was in deep trouble, he called out to the Lord for help (Psalm 28:1–2). Afterward, he remembered to give God thanks for delivering him (vv. 6–7). In fact, David's heart of gratitude toward the Lord is evident throughout the book of Psalms.

What about us? Do we have an ungrateful response to the Lord's graciousness? Or are we, like David, unceasingly expressing our thanks to God for His goodness?

—David Egner

———

The reason for the psalmist's praise in Psalm 30:12 relates to the beautiful phrase "you turned my wailing into dancing" (v. 11). Deliverance—what a majestic gift from God!

OUR BEST DEFENSE

Read: Psalm 31:1-8

Be my rock of refuge, a strong fortress to save me. —PSALM 31:2

In late January 1956, during the tense days of the Montgomery Boycott, civil rights leader Dr. Martin Luther King Jr. could not sleep. A threatening phone call had terrified him. So he prayed, "I am here taking a stand for what I believe is right. But Lord, I must confess that I'm weak now, I'm faltering. I'm losing my courage. Now, I am afraid. . . . The people are looking to me for leadership, and if I stand before them without strength and courage, they too will falter. I am at the end of my powers. . . . I can't face it alone."

Dr. King later wrote, "At that moment I experienced the presence of the Divine as I never experienced Him before. It seemed as though I could hear the quiet assurance of an inner voice saying, 'Stand up for righteousness, stand up for truth; and God will be at your side forever.' Almost at once my fears began to go. My uncertainty disappeared. I was ready to face anything."

The rest is history. Dr. King wanted to see people of all colors free of the damage done by racism and prejudice.

If we face opposition when we're trying to do what's right, we too must cry out to the Lord. He alone is our "rock of refuge, a strong fortress" (Psalm 31:2). He is our reliable source of strength and protection.

—*David Egner*

David knew the importance of a "rock of refuge" and a "strong fortress" as he recalled the times he was pursued by the delusional King Saul. David learned firsthand that his only safety was God.

҉

COVER-UPS STINK

Blessed is the one whose transgressions are forgiven, whose sins are covered.
—PSALM 32:1

The smell at an overflowing garbage landfill became a growing public concern. So workers installed high-pressured deodorant guns to counteract the smell. The cannons could spray several gallons of fragrance a minute over a distance of up to 50 yards across the mounds of putrefying garbage. However, no matter how many gallons of deodorant are sprayed to mask the odorous rubbish, the fragrance will serve only as a cover-up until the source of the stench is removed.

King David tried a cover-up as well. After his adultery with Bathsheba, he attempted to use silence, deceit, and piety to mask his moral failures (2 Samuel 11–12). In Psalm 32 he talks about experiencing the intense convicting hand of God when he remained silent (vv. 3–4). Unable to withstand the conviction any longer, David uncovered his sin by acknowledging, confessing, and repenting of it (v. 5). He no longer needed to cover it because God forgave him.

It's futile to try to hide our sin. The stench of our disobedience will seep through whatever we use to try to cover it. Let's acknowledge to God the rubbish in our hearts and experience the fresh cleansing of His grace and forgiveness.

—*Marvin Williams*

How can we not be "blessed," or "happy," as some render this word, when we remember that God not only forgives us through Jesus, but also pushes our sins away—out of our sight—as far as the east is from the west?

LET'S SING!

Read: Psalm 33:1-11

Sing joyfully to the LORD, you righteous; it is fitting for the upright to praise him. . . . Sing to him a new song. —PSALM 33:1–3

Singing has always played a vital role in the worship of God. The psalms were sung in the temple, often in the form of beautiful antiphons; that is, responses between a soloist and the choir, then between the choir and the worshipers. Jesus and His disciples sang a hymn after He had instituted the Lord's Supper (Matthew 26:30). Paul encouraged believers to address one another with "psalms, hymns, and songs from the Spirit" (Ephesians 5:19).

Why should God's people sing? We sing because it is an effective way to express our adoration, our supplication, or our testimony. Through song we praise our God and edify one another.

The writer of Psalm 33 called upon the worshiping Israelites to sing praise to God for His powerful word, His unfailing counsels, and His continual concern for His people. Paul and Silas, in prison with their feet in stocks and their backs raw from a brutal flogging, sang because they were filled with the joy of salvation.

If you truly love the Lord, join enthusiastically with others in praising Him through song. When you're all alone and your heart is full, sing! Don't worry about how it sounds. The Lord is pleased with any melody of praise that comes from the heart.

—Herb Vander Lugt

If we look back in chapter 32, we read of the psalmist's joy because of the Lord's mercy: "Rejoice in the LORD and be glad, you righteous; sing, all you who are upright in heart!" (v. 11). Does our life demonstrate that kind of joy?

THE LAST JELLYBEAN

Read: Psalm 34:1-10

Taste and see that the LORD is good . . . . Those who seek the LORD lack no good thing. —PSALM 34:8, 10

One afternoon Angela gave her young daughter four jellybeans and let her know that was all the candy she was going to receive.

After practically inhaling the first three candies, Eliana lingered over the final one. She sucked on it, took it out of her mouth, bit into it, sucked on it some more, then gnawed at the outer shell. Knowing that this was her last jellybean, she took a full 45 minutes to ingest the treat completely.

Angela observed her little girl with amusement. It occurred to her that she was watching Eliana learn the value of savoring—enjoying taste and texture and learning to draw out every possible bit of flavor from the pleasurable experience.

When we read, "Taste and see that the LORD is good" (Psalm 34:8), we can be sure that God wants us to "savor" His presence. He allows us to gain intimate and satisfying knowledge of Him. And when we meditate on His Word, we will draw out a deeper understanding of who He is (Ezekiel 3:1–3). As we taste His goodness and love, He will reveal the distinctive flavor of His creativity, sovereignty, holiness, and faithfulness.

Our Father must look on with enjoyment as we learn how to enjoy and savor Him.

—*Cindy Hess Kasper*

The apostle Peter used the imagery of Psalm 34:8 to encourage young Christians to grow in maturity (1 Peter 2:2-3). A growing maturity seems to be at hand for those who taste, trust, and fear the Lord (Psalm 34:8-9).

JUST YOU AND GOD

Read: Psalm 36:5-9

How precious is Your lovingkindness, O God! Therefore the children of men put their trust under the shadow of Your wings.
—PSALM 36:7 (NKJV)

One spring a pair of blue jays built a nest in the persimmon tree in our backyard. I enjoyed watching the mother bird as she sat patiently on her eggs. In a matter of days, I noticed a new development. The father would fly in, the mother would perch on the side of that little home, and four little mouths could be seen gaping above the edge of the nest. To get a better look, I would edge closer to the tree. Then I would stand very still and watch the mother. When I got too close, however, she would spread her wings over her little brood. Her head would cautiously protrude as she looked first to one side and then to the other. She was always on guard, protecting her little ones by sheltering them with her wings.

This beautiful picture of protection reminds me of David's words in Psalm 36:7. When he said we can find safety "in the shadow of [God's] wings," he may have been referring to the words of his ancestor Boaz (Ruth 2:12). Boaz had said to Ruth, "May the LORD repay you for what you have done. May you be richly rewarded by the LORD, the God of Israel, under whose wings you have come to take refuge."

Surely that's a promise we still need. Life is filled with dangers, both physical and spiritual. Yet, we can rest securely because we know that God is aware of them all. What better refuge could we have than to live under the shadow of His wings!

—*Paul Van Gorder*

Think about what the word *precious* (v. 7 NKJV) indicates. When we consider something to be *precious*, it takes on a closeness, an intimacy. God in His unfailing love is close enough for us to huddle under His protection.

THE LAST WORD

Read: Psalm 38:9-22

I am like the deaf, who cannot hear, like the mute, who cannot speak.
—PSALM 38:13

Walter Heller tells of an experience he had while speaking to the Independent Banker's Association in Denver. In the middle of his talk, a man way in the back suddenly hollered out, "You're stupid!" About five minutes later the man shouted again, "You're stupid!" Heller was irritated. Noticing a slight slur in his voice, he thought, "I'll be ready for him the next time."

Before Heller finished his speech, the man shouted for a third time, "You're stupid!" Heller was quick to reply, "And you're drunk!" The detractor responded, "Yes, but tomorrow I will be sober and you will still be stupid."

Returning insult for insult only makes matters worse. How much better to respond as David did to his enemies! He was sick because he had sinned, and he was vulnerable (Psalm 38:1–5). His loved ones, relatives, and friends had deserted him (v. 11), and his enemies were seeking to harm him (vv. 12, 19–20). Instead of lashing out at them, he turned a deaf ear to what they were saying about him and put his hope in the Lord (vv. 13–15).

Father, help us to be as wise as David. Help us to maintain dignity by trusting you when others take unfair advantage of us. Help us to restrain ourselves and let you have the last word.

—*Mart DeHaan*

There are times when our answer
will not effectively silence our enemies.
At such times, we can thankfully
turn to the Lord and His Word.

�҉

JOY IN THE MORNING

Read: Psalm 40:1-5

Weeping may stay for the night, but rejoicing comes in the morning.
—PSALM 30:5

Angie could not see through the fogged-up windows in her car. Inadvertently, she pulled out in front of a truck. The accident caused such damage to her brain that she could no longer speak or take care of herself.

Over the years, I have been amazed at the resiliency of Angie's parents. Recently I asked them, "How have you managed to get through this experience?" Her father thoughtfully responded, "In all honesty, the only way we have been able to do this is by drawing close to God. He gives us the strength we need to help us through."

Angie's mother agreed and added that around the time of the accident, their grieving was so deep that they wondered if they would ever have joy again. As they both leaned upon God, they experienced countless unexpected provisions for the physical and spiritual care of Angie and their entire family. Although Angie may never regain her ability to speak, she now responds to them with wide smiles, and this gives them joy. Her parents' favorite verse continues to be: "Weeping may stay for the night, but rejoicing comes in the morning" (Psalm 30:5).

Have you experienced extreme sorrow? There is the promise of future joy amid your tears as you lean upon our loving Lord.

—*Dennis Fisher*

As Psalm 40 begins, David is in a "slimy pit," and we can say, "Been there, done that." But he concludes, "You are my help and my deliverer" (v. 17). Weeping weighs us down, but the joy of the Lord lifts our hearts "in the morning" (30:5).

"IT NEVER TOUCHED
MY HEART"

Read: Psalm 41

*The LORD sustains them on their sickbed and restores them
from their bed of illness.* —PSALM 41:3

I suppose there are people who have never known affliction. But for most of us, sickness—whether physical, mental, or emotional—crowds into our lives sooner or later. The natural and proper response is to seek relief. The Bible does not guarantee a life free from illness or disability, nor does it assure us that every prayer for recovery will be answered—though many are. But it does promise a spiritual wholeness.

This is illustrated by a story about a handicapped high school student. Although the crutches he had to use kept him from being physically active, he excelled in his studies and was well liked by his peers. For a long time nobody asked him why he needed crutches. One day, however, his closest friend finally did. "It was polio," answered the student. The friend responded, "With so many difficulties, how do you keep from becoming bitter?" Tapping his chest with his hand, the young man replied with a smile, "Oh, it never touched my heart."

If you are a Christian who is suffering from a long-term illness that God has not seen fit to remove, don't give in to bitterness, rebellion, self-pity, or guilt. When those emotions well up, as they surely will, be honest with God. He understands. As long as you keep your life open to Him, your affliction will never touch your heart.

—Dennis DeHaan

———

In this psalm, an illness afflicts David—something that relates to his own sin, it seems. Even his close friend rejects him (v. 9), yet the Lord continues to sustain him.

REALLY THIRSTY

Read: Psalm 42

As the deer pants for streams of water, so my soul pants for you, my God.
—PSALM 42:1

Have you ever been really thirsty?

Years ago, I visited my sister Kathy in Mali, West Africa. During an afternoon of seeing the sights, the temperature had risen far above 100° F. Parched, I told her, "Hey, I need something to drink." When Kathy told me she had forgotten to bring along a supply of filtered water, I began to get a bit desperate. The longer we drove, the more I wondered what it was like to truly die of thirst.

Finally, Kathy said, "I know where we can go," as she drove up to the gate of an embassy. Inside I beheld the most beautiful sight—a water cooler! I grabbed one of the tiny paper cups and filled it again and again. My body had been deprived too long and now required lots of liquid to reverse the effects of dehydration.

The psalmist compared physical thirst with spiritual thirst: "As the deer pants for streams of water, so my soul pants for you, my God" (Psalm 42:1). His thirst was that of a desperate longing for God—the one and only "living God" (v. 2).

Do you long for something this world can't provide? This dissatisfaction is a thirst of the soul for God. Run to the One who alone can quench that thirst. "He satisfies the thirsty, and fills the hungry with good things" (Psalm 107:9).

—*Cindy Hess Kasper*

Many things can distance us from God, but the only answer for the great thirst we feel as a result is in searching and finding a place to again "meet with God" and drink in our fellowship with Him.

GOD'S WHEELCHAIR

Read: Psalm 46

God is our refuge and strength, an ever-present help in trouble.
—PSALM 46:1

Jean Driscoll is a remarkable athlete. She has won the Boston Marathon eight times. She has also participated in four Paralympic Games and won five gold medals. Born with spina bifida, Jean competes in a wheelchair.

One of Driscoll's favorite Bible verses is Daniel 7:9, "The Ancient of Days took his seat. . . . His throne was flaming with fire, and its wheels were all ablaze." Seeing a connection between Daniel's vision of God and her own situation, she is able to pass along words of encouragement to others. "Anytime I've had an opportunity to talk with people who use wheelchairs and feel bad about being in a chair, I tell them, 'Not only are you made in the image of God, but your wheelchair is made in the image of His throne!' "

Daniel's vision, of course, doesn't portray God as being impaired in motion. In fact, some see God's "wheelchair" as a symbol of a just God sovereignly moving within human affairs. Other passages speak of God's providence providing help to those who believe (Proverbs 3:25–26; Matthew 20:29–34; Ephesians 1:11).

Jean Driscoll's faith in God has helped her triumph over personal challenges. We too can be confident that the high and holy One is near and ready to help us if only we ask, because that is exactly what we are told in Psalm 46.

—*Dennis Fisher*

God's power is evident in Psalm 46. Here we see that He has power over the elements (vv. 1–30), power over attackers (v. 6), and power over warring nations (vv. 8–9). Indeed, the "God of Jacob is our fortress" (v. 11).

PLENTY TO PRAISE

Read: Psalm 48

Great is the LORD, and most worthy of praise. —PSALM 48:1

God. Have you ever just sat back and marveled at how grand and glorious He is? Today, let's pause to ponder His majesty and greatness.

To help us do that, here are a few descriptions of God that I found while reading Psalms 1–48.

The Lord is a shield (3:3), my source of safety (4:8), my King (5:2), the Judge (7:8), the Most High (7:17), my refuge (9:9), the helper of the fatherless (10:14), the King forever (10:16), righteous (11:7).

God is my strength, rock, fortress, stronghold (18:1–3; 28:1; 31:4), my deliverer (18:2), my support (18:18), my Redeemer (19:14).

He is my shepherd (23:1), the King of glory (24:7), the Lord of hosts (24:10), the God of my salvation (25:5), my light and my salvation (27:1), my strength and shield (27:1; 28:7).

He is the God of glory (29:3), the Lord God of truth (31:5), the living God (42:2), my help in trouble (46:1), the King over all the earth (47:2).

That should be enough to meditate on for one day.

No, that's enough for an eternity! He is "our God for ever and ever" (48:14).

Let's start today to worship our God in earnest—the One who gives us so many reasons to praise Him.

—*Dave Branon*

The focus of Psalm 48 is on the greatness of God toward Jerusalem. God has protected His city from its adversaries. We too have reason for praising God, for He is our "God for ever" and "will be our guide even to the end" (v. 14).

✗

WEAK BENEATH THE SURFACE

Read: Psalm 49:6-15

Surely the lowborn are but a breath, the highborn are but a lie.
—PSALM 62:9

In 1835 a man visited a doctor in Florence, Italy. He was filled with anxiety and exhausted from lack of sleep. He couldn't eat, and he avoided his friends. The doctor examined him and found that he was in prime physical condition. Concluding that his patient needed to have a good time, the physician told him about a circus in town and its star performer, a clown named Grimaldi. Night after night he had the people rolling in the aisles. "You must go and see him," the doctor advised. "Grimaldi is the world's funniest clown. He'll make you laugh and cure your sadness." "No," replied the despairing man, "he can't help me. You see, I am Grimaldi!"

Many people are like that clown—weak beneath the surface. The psalmist refers to them as having riches and honor and as giving the appearance of confidence and strength. Yet they lack spiritual understanding and will perish like the animals (Psalm 49:12–14).

We see this even today. People appear to be something they aren't. In front of the cameras, behind the desk, or dressed in their finest clothes, they are pictures of strength. But let's not kid ourselves; we are all made of the same flesh, and apart from the grace and power of God we are helpless and pathetic. Only by yielding to the Holy Spirit can we find the inner resources we need.

Are you displaying His power, or are you wearing a mask that covers weakness beneath the surface?

—*Mart DeHaan*

In verses 13-15, the psalmist contrasts the temporary riches that lead to nothingness with the eternal riches of redemption.

THE VOICE OF GOD AT SUNSET

Read: Psalm 50

The Mighty One, God, the LORD, speaks and summons the earth from the rising of the sun to where it sets. —PSALM 50:1

Who has not marveled at the beauty of a sunset? We stand motionless, awestruck, hushed by the flaming sky as the sun moves over the western horizon. Seeming to hesitate a moment, the glowing orb suddenly drops out of sight, leaving the sky ablaze with brilliant shades of pink, orange, and red. Somehow the frustrations of the day are put to silence by the majestic, yet soothing voice of God as we view a glorious sunset.

Because the sun's rays are slowed down slightly and bent by the earth's atmosphere, the sun appears to be oval-shaped rather than round. That, along with the dust or smog in the air, explains the dazzling array of colors that give us so much visual pleasure at day's end. And scientists tell us that a sunset can be even more beautiful than most of us have seen. Writing in the *Encyclopedia Science Supplement,* astronomer John B. Irwin said, "When conditions are just right, the last diminishing bit of the yellow-orange sun suddenly changes into a brilliant emerald green. This green flash puts an exciting exclamation point to the end of the day."

To Christians, every sunset is an exclamation point given to us by God the Creator to end the day. It's as if the Lord were saying, "Set aside your worries. Rest from your labors. I am still here, taking care of My universe. I am in control. Look up beyond the sun to Me and be at peace." No wonder the psalmist spoke of the voice of God at sunset!

—*David Egner*

As God appears to swoop onto the scene, He is given three designations. He is "the Mighty One," He is "God," and He is "the LORD." Contemplate all that this means.

THE WONDER OF GRACE

Read: Psalm 51

My sacrifice, O God, is a broken spirit; a broken and contrite heart you, God, will not despise. —PSALM 51:17

When I was a young boy, a few of my friends had fathers who led their families in daily Bible reading and never missed a church service. But I also knew that some of them were proud, tyrants at home, ruthless in their business dealings, and heartless toward people in need. Even as a youngster, I realized that this kind of hypocrisy did not please God.

I was grateful that my father and several other men I knew modeled true faith and humility. They were quick to admit their wrongs and treated others with compassion. They obviously saw themselves as unworthy recipients of God's wonderful grace.

In Psalm 51, David expressed his deep sense of guilt and his desperate need for God's forgiveness and cleansing. As he grieved over his sin, he came to the Lord with the sacrifice of "a broken and contrite heart" (v. 17). When David thought about God's love, mercy, and grace, he was filled with gratitude and praise.

If we recognize the seriousness of our sin, we too will come to the Lord with the sacrifice of "a broken and a contrite heart." As we consider what Jesus did for us on the cross, taking the full punishment for all our sins, then we will be overwhelmed with the wonder of grace.

—Herb Vander Lugt

———

This penitential psalm of David allows us to listen in as he grieves his own sins and pleads with God for forgiveness. The contrast between David's sin and God's grace is a strong reminder for all of us to keep our accounts clear with Him.

A FOOL'S ARGUMENT

Read: Psalm 53

The fool says in his heart, "There is no God." —PSALM 53:1

Some people spend a great deal of time and effort trying to disprove the existence of God. By doing so, however, they undermine their own arguments. In *Interpreting Basic Theology*, Addison Leitch wrote, "Unless [an atheist] is carrying on his fight against absolute nothingness—and this makes us wonder about his zeal—then he must be [arguing] against something he finds ingrained in himself and in others."

This inherent belief in God doesn't prove He exists, but it strongly hints in that direction. When C. S. Lewis was an atheist, he rejected the idea of a divine Being because of all the injustice in the world. But when he asked himself where he had gotten the idea of justice in the first place, he had a problem. "Man doesn't call a line crooked unless he has some idea of a straight line," wrote Lewis. "What was I comparing this universe with when I called it unjust?" Lewis realized that his case for atheism was too simple. If the idea of justice were merely a product of his own imagination, that would have destroyed his argument, which depended on real injustices. Injustice in the world, in fact, pointed to a God who himself set the standard of justice.

The fool says there is no God (Psalm 53:1). So be wise instead and make it your primary goal to love the God who is there.

—*Dennis DeHaan*

Psalm 53 closely mirrors Psalm 14. One major difference is in verse 5. Another difference is that God is called Elohim in Psalm 53 and Yahweh in Psalm 14.

GIVE HIM YOUR BURDEN

Read: Psalm 55:16-23

Cast your cares on the LORD, and he will sustain you. —PSALM 55:22

A poor man in Ireland was plodding along toward home, carrying a huge bag of potatoes. A horse and wagon finally drew up alongside him on the road, and the driver invited the man to climb aboard. After getting on the wagon, he sat down but continued to hold the heavy bag.

When the driver suggested that the man set the bag down in the wagon, he replied, "I don't want to trouble you too much, sir. You are giving me a ride already, so I'll just carry the potatoes."

"How foolish of him!" we say. Yet sometimes we do the same thing when we attempt to bear the burdens of our lives in our own strength. No wonder we become weary and overwhelmed with anxiety and fear.

In Psalm 55, David spoke of the anxiety he felt because his enemies were attacking him (vv. 1–15). But then he gave his concerns to the Lord and was filled with renewed hope and confidence (vv. 16–23). That's why he could write, "Cast your cares on the LORD, and he will sustain you" (v. 22).

When you recall the story of the man and his bag of potatoes, remember the simple lesson it illustrates: Rather than trying to bear your burdens by yourself, set them down in God's hands.

—Henry Bosch

Just as Daniel prayed three times
a day when he was in exile in Babylon,
the writer of Psalm 55 prayed three times
a day for God's help (v. 17).
We can learn about persistence
in prayer through their examples.

✕

WHEN FEAR CREEPS IN

Read: Psalm 56

When I am afraid, I put my trust in [God]. —PSALM 56:3

When my daughter exclaimed, "Mommy, a bug!" I looked where she was pointing and saw the largest spider I have ever encountered outside of a pet shop. Both the spider and I knew that he would not be allowed to stay in our house. And yet, as I faced him, I found I could not take one step closer to end the standoff. My pulse quickened. I swallowed and gave myself a pep talk. Still, fear kept me frozen in place.

Fear is powerful; it can override logical thinking and produce irrational behavior. Thankfully, Christians don't have to let fear of anything—people, situations, or even spiders—rule our actions. We can declare, "When I am afraid, I put my trust in [God]" (Psalm 56:3).

Taking this stand against fear is consistent with the Bible's instruction to "trust in the LORD with all your heart and lean not on your own understanding" (Proverbs 3:5). Our own understanding may lead us to overestimate the object of our fear and underestimate God's power. When we are afraid, we can depend on God's understanding (Isaiah 40:28) and trust in His love for us that "drives out fear" (1 John 4:18). The next time fear creeps into your life, don't panic. God can be trusted in the darkness.

—*Jennifer Benson Schuldt*

In this psalm, David is probably referring to a situation recorded in 1 Samuel 21:12 when he feared for his life at the hands of Achish, king of Gath. He truly was afraid.

SNAPPING, SNARLING THOUGHTS

Read: Psalm 59

You are my fortress, my refuge in times of trouble. —PSALM 59:16

Many years ago, my father and I hiked through Big Bend in Texas. It's a national park now, but in those days it was rough country.

One night we were rolling out our sleeping bags when a couple with a dog asked if they could camp nearby. We welcomed their company and turned in for the night. They tethered their dog to a stake beside their tent.

Some hours later my father nudged me awake and turned his flashlight into the darkness. Illuminated by the light, we saw pairs of yellow eyes peering out of the shadows. A pack of snapping and snarling coyotes were closing in on the dog. Although we chased them off and our neighbors put the dog in their tent, we slept fitfully.

I think of that night when I read Psalm 59 and David's twice-repeated imagery: "They return at evening, snarling like dogs" (vv. 6, 14). David was thinking of Saul's army that was closing in on him. I think, however, of the thoughts that return to menace us. They come back at nightfall, snapping and snarling: "You're stupid." "You're a failure." "You're useless." "Who needs you?"

When we have such thoughts, we can revel in God's unconditional, unending love. His steady devotion is our refuge in the dark night of self-doubt and fear (v. 16).

—*David Roper*

This psalm depicts King Saul's dogged pursuit of David. Here Saul's men rise up against David—lying in wait. Like vicious dogs, they come after him. Yet David knows that the Lord is his "fortress" and "refuge in times of trouble."

FILLING UP EMPTY

Read: Psalm 62

Do not trust in extortion or put vain hope in stolen goods; though your riches increase, do not set your heart on them. —PSALM 62:10

"This house ain't worth robbing," said a thief who seemed to feel he was wasting his time. According to a news report, the burglar broke into a home and held the owner at knifepoint while looking for money. He ransacked the place but turned up only $3 in change, $5 in a wallet, and a few pieces of cheap jewelry.

The thief apparently concluded that the homeowner was worse off than he was, so he gave back to him the $8 he was going to steal. "I think he was disgusted," said the 32-year-old victim. "He couldn't believe that was all the money I had."

We might smile at the bad fortune of this thief. But we can often have a similar kind of experience. It happens whenever we try to take something that God has not given us. Following the path of envy, jealousy, adultery, theft (Psalm 62:10), or just plain stubborn willfulness, always results in more trouble than profit.

David, the psalmist, learned this the hard way. When he stole Uriah's wife, he ended up with far more trouble and far less happiness than he had bargained for (2 Samuel 11–12).

Father, help us to believe that it never pays to take what you have not given. Help us not to waste our lives chasing things that leave you out and leave us empty.

—*Mart DeHaan*

———

Bible scholar Derek Kidner suggests that Psalm 62:10 is referenced by Paul in 1 Timothy 6:17, which says, "Command those who are rich in this present world not to be arrogant nor to put their hope in wealth, which is so uncertain, but to put their hope in God."

EAT FAST, PAY LESS

Read: Psalm 63:1-8

I thirst for you, my whole being longs for you. —PSALM 63:1

A hotel in Singapore introduced an express buffet—eat all you can in 30 minutes and pay just half the price! After that experience, one diner reported: "I lost my decorum, stuffing my mouth with yet more food. I lost my civility, . . . and I lost my appetite for the rest of the day, so severe was my heartburn."

Sometimes I think in our devotional reading we treat God's Word like an express buffet. We wolf it down as fast as we can and wonder why we haven't learned very much. Like physical food, spiritual food needs chewing! For those of us who have been Christians for a long time, we may have a tendency to speed-read through the passages we've read many times before. But in doing so, we miss what God is meaning to show us. One sure sign of this is when we learn nothing new from that passage.

David's desire was right when he wrote in Psalm 119:15, "I meditate on your precepts and consider your ways." That's the way to treat God's Word—to take time to mull it over.

Let's not come to the Bible as if we were going to an express buffet. Only by meditating on God's Word will we get the most value for our spiritual well-being.

—*C. P. Hia*

In Psalm 63:6, the secret to properly taking in the essence of God and His Word comes into focus: "I meditate on You in the night watches" (NKJV). The word translated *meditate* here has the meaning to not only consider but also to "mutter" or "speak of." It's more than just thinking about God. It's also speaking of Him.

SQUIRREL FEEDER

Read: Psalm 65

You crown the year with your bounty, and your carts overflow with abundance. —PSALM 65:11

Some years ago I placed a squirrel feeder on a fir tree a few yards from our home. It's a simple device—two boards and a nail on which to impale a corncob. Each morning a squirrel comes to enjoy that day's meal. She's a pretty thing—black with a round, gray tummy.

I sit on our back porch in the morning and watch her eat. She plucks each kernel from the cob, holds it in her paws, turns it around and eats the heart out of the kernel. At the end of the day no kernels remain, only a neat little pile of leftovers under the tree.

Despite my care for her, the creature is afraid of me. When I approach, she runs away, taking refuge in her tree and chattering at me when I get too close. She doesn't know that I provide for her.

Some people are like that with God. They run from Him in fear. They don't know that He loves them and richly provides them with everything for their enjoyment (Psalm 65:11).

Henry Scougal, a seventeenth-century Scottish minister, wrote, "Nothing is more powerful to engage our affection than to find that we are [loved by] One who is altogether lovely . . . . How must this astonish and delight us; how must it overcome our [fear] and melt our hearts." God's love is the perfect love that "drives out fear" (1 John 4:18).

—*David Roper*

What a neat picture David gives us
of God's goodness dripping abundance
upon us—a picture of God's cornucopia
of provisions spilling out into our lives—
just because He loves us.

)(

WORSHIP BY PRAYER

Read: Psalm 66

Shout for joy to God, all the earth! —PSALM 66:1

When was the last time you and God met together for a worship service? No choir. No piano. No order of service. Just you and God and prayer.

Want an example? Listen to the psalmist: "I cried to [the Lord] with my mouth; his praise was on my tongue. If I had cherished sin in my heart, the Lord would not have listened; but God has surely listened and has heard my prayer. Praise be to God, who has not rejected my prayer or withheld his love from me!" (Psalm 66:17–20).

Did you notice what was happening in those verses? The psalmist called out to God in praise. He came with a pure heart—cleansed by confession. He was confident that God was listening. God accepted the prayer, and He lavished His love on the person praying. The psalmist's worship included praise, a pure heart, and communicating with God; and then God's affirmation and love were poured out. Yes, true worship took place.

What a pattern! Think of the spiritual advantage you gain and the honor God receives when you practice worship by prayer. Anytime, anyplace, you can worship the Lord, and He will bless you.

Are you ready to worship?

—*Dave Branon*

———

In verse 5, the psalmist says, "Come and see what God has done" and then recaps Israel's glorious victories from God's hands. This verse applies to our lives as well in so many ways. Come and see!

PIGS DON'T PRAY

Read: Psalm 68:4-10

Praise be to the Lord, to God our Savior, who daily bears our burdens.
—PSALM 68:19

A Christian farmer went to the city on business and stopped at a small restaurant for lunch. When his food was served, he bowed his head and gave God thanks, just as he always did at home. A young fellow at the next table noticed that the farmer was praying. Thinking that he was a little backward and not in touch with "city ways," he asked loudly to embarrass him, "Say, farmer, does everyone do that out in the country where you live?" The earnest Christian turned to him and replied kindly, "No, son, the pigs don't."

The more I observe people, the more I notice that it is the exception rather than the rule to see people bow and give thanks to God in public. We seem to have become a very self-indulgent and ungrateful society.

In Psalm 68, David reviewed the many ways God had cared for His people Israel. After surveying Jehovah's faithfulness, he exclaimed, "Praise be to the Lord, to God our Savior, who daily bears our burdens." From a heart overflowing with love for the Lord, David gave thanks often. Should we not respond in like manner for every blessing God has so freely given? Shouldn't we express to Him our gratitude at all times?

Let's remember to say thanks to God for our daily supply of blessings—even in a crowded restaurant. Let's not be like the pigs.

—*Paul Van Gorder*

Some have translated the phrase "daily bears our burdens" to mean "daily loads us with benefits." Both are true. God lightens our load of burdens and provides us with all we need—every day!

THE OTHER EIGHTY PERCENT

Read: Psalm 69:29-36

Let heaven and earth praise him, the seas and all that move in them.
—PSALM 69:34

Recently I saw a billboard stating that 80 percent of all life on Earth is found in the seas. That staggering number is difficult to process, largely because most of that life is out of sight.

As I considered this, it reminded me of how much greater God's creation is than we typically appreciate. While we can easily have our breath taken away by a majestic mountain range or a panoramic sunset, we sometimes fail to see His extraordinary work in the details that require more careful study and examination. Not only is much of God's creation hidden by the oceans, but other parts are also too small for our eyes to observe. From the microscopically small to the unsearched reaches of the universe, it is all the work of our Creator. In those magnificent structures—seen and unseen—God's creative glory is revealed (Romans 1:20).

As we grow to understand the wonder of creation, it must always point us to the Creator himself—and call us to worship Him. As the psalmist said, "Let heaven and earth praise him, the seas and all that move in them" (Psalm 69:34). If creation itself gives praise to the Creator, we can and should certainly join the chorus. What a mighty God we serve!

—*Bill Crowder*

Deliverance is in sight for David as he sees ahead to Israel's future. Like him, we can look ahead to see God's ultimate deliverance for us—a rescue that will put us in the ultimate Holy City, New Jerusalem (Revelation 21:2).

WHEN LIFE SEEMS UNFAIR

Read: Psalm 73

I envied the arrogant when I saw the prosperity of the wicked.
—PSALM 73:3

Have you ever felt that life is unfair? For those of us who are committed to following the will and ways of Jesus, it's easy to get frustrated when people who don't care about Him seem to do well in life. A businessman cheats yet wins a large contract, and the guy who parties all the time is robust and healthy—while you or your loved ones struggle with finances or medical issues. It makes us feel cheated, like maybe we've been good for nothing.

If you've ever felt that way, you're in good company. The writer of Psalm 73 goes through a whole list of how the wicked prosper, and then he says, "Surely in vain I have kept my heart pure" (v. 13). But the tide of his thoughts turns when he recalls his time in God's presence: "Then I understood their final destiny" (v. 17).

When we spend time with God and see things from His point of view, it changes our perspective completely. We may be jealous of nonbelievers now, but we won't be at judgment time. As the saying goes, what difference does it make if you win the battle but lose the war?

Like the psalmist, let's praise God for His presence in this life and His promise of the life to come (vv. 25–28). He is all you need, even when life seems unfair.

—*Joe Stowell*

Isn't the writer expressing what we have all thought at one time or another—that God should, as H. C. Leupold puts it, "reward the godly with tokens of His favor and punish the wicked"? When we get caught up in this kind of faulty thinking, let's do as Asaph did and enter "the sanctuary of God" (v. 17).

LIKE A FLOCK

Read: Psalm 77:11-20

You led your people like a flock by the hand of Moses and Aaron.
—PSALM 77:20

During a demonstration of sheepherding using a Border Col-lie, the dog trainer explained that because sheep are highly vulnerable to wild animals, their main defense against preda-tors is to stay together in a tightly knit group. "A sheep alone is a dead sheep," the trainer said. "The dog always keeps the sheep together as it moves them."

The biblical image of God as our shepherd is a powerful reminder of how much we need each other in the community of faith. When writing about the exodus of the Israelites from Egypt, the psalmist said, "[God] brought his people out like a flock; he led them like sheep through the wilderness. He guided them safely, so they were unafraid" (Psalm 78:52–53).

As part of God's flock, we who have trusted Christ are under His guiding, protecting hand while being surrounded by the shielding presence of others. We are part of a larger body of believers in which there is safety and accountability.

While we don't give up our personal responsibility for thought and action as members of the flock, we are to embrace the concept of "we" rather than "me" in our daily lives. With Christ as our Shepherd and with fellow believers around us, we find safety in the flock.

—*David McCasland*

While God was the true Shepherd
who led His people on their wilderness
journey, Psalm 77:20 reminds us that God
used undershepherds along the way—
and we can be thankful for
their guidance as well.

ᚷ

TELL THE CHILDREN

Read: Psalm 78:1-8

We will tell the next generation the praiseworthy deeds of the LORD.
—PSALM 78:4

Imagine an evening in ancient Israel. The day's work is done, the meal is finished, and the family is gathered around a small fire that pushes away the night chill and casts a soft glow on their faces. It's story time.

Father and grandfather take turns relating to the children the "praiseworthy deeds of the LORD" (Psalm 78:4). They tell of Abraham's journey. They speak of Isaac. Their voices come alive when they tell about old Jacob. They remember Moses and Joshua and Elijah and the great King David. They recount the history of their own family. And all the time they focus their attention on the mighty works of God on behalf of His people.

That's the way Jewish men fulfilled their responsibility to tell the next generation about the Lord: They had been told by their parents, who had been told by their parents.

Our children need to know about God. They need to learn from us about His love, His faithfulness, and His grace. They need to hear from us about the times He stepped into our lives to protect and provide.

So gather up your sons and daughters and grandchildren. Relate to them how God has worked in your life. Fulfill your responsibility, and tell the children.

—David Egner

This psalm doesn't present a new concept. Deuteronomy 6:7 is one of several times in the Bible when the Israelites were told to keep telling the story of God to their children—a teaching that definitely transfers to us.

DO YOU LIVE IN A BOX?

Read: Psalm 84

The LORD bestows favor and honor; no good thing does he withhold from those whose walk is blameless. —PSALM 84:11

Incredible as it sounds, Alexander Whortley lived in a mini-trailer three feet wide, four feet long, and five feet high until he died at the age of eighty. It was made of wood, had a metal roof, and it housed him and all his meager belongings. No matter where he worked, Whortley chose to spend his life in that cramped space, even though larger quarters were always available.

I can't imagine why anyone would choose to live in a box—certainly not if housing with far more elbowroom were available. But are we allowing ourselves to be squeezed into narrow boxes of a different sort? Are we hemmed in by selfishness, an unforgiving spirit, bitterness, or sinful habits? Are we boxed in by unbelief with its coffinlike narrowness of vision, seeing only this little world and this brief lifetime as the hope-suffocating sum of our existence?

God wants us to live in the expansive joy of His strength, realizing the security of His protection and the blessing of His favor (Psalm 84:11). He lovingly urges us to dwell in the spacious mansion of faith and freedom in Jesus Christ. But to do this, we must, in obedience to the Lord, move out of our spiritual boxes and abandon the doubt, the guilt, and the fear that constrict our souls.

—Vernon Grounds

In Psalm 84:11, the psalmist gives a qualifier for God's blessings. Notice the converse of this truth in Jeremiah 5:25 where the prophet warns Judah: "Your sins have deprived you of good."

BULL'S-EYE

Read: Psalm 86

Teach me your way, LORD, that I may rely on your faithfulness.
—PSALM 86:11

If we're not careful, we may become like the man who prided himself on being an expert archer. The secret to his success was that after he shot his arrow at the side of a barn, he painted a bull's-eye around the arrow.

It's easy to live our lives doing what we want and thinking that our ways and instincts are right on target when in reality our "bull's-eye" shots at life are not on target at all. Proverbs 14:12 says, "There is a way that appears to be right, but in the end it leads to death."

Sometimes it may feel right to seek revenge, hoard money, chase pleasure, or yell at people who yell at us. But God's ways are different from ours. He has painted a bull's-eye on forgiving those who have hurt us, on giving generously to those in need, on living to please Him rather than ourselves, and on turning the other cheek. We need to pray, "Teach me your way, LORD, that I may rely on your faithfulness" (Psalm 86:11). And then we need to aim to follow His ways in all that we do and say.

But we all need help to aim at the right target. Thankfully, the bull's-eye is already painted in the brushstrokes of God's truth as revealed in His Word. When we aim our lives at God's Word, we'll discover that His ways are right on target—every time!

—*Joe Stowell*

___

Sanctification is an ongoing process for the believer. Notice that David says to God in verse 2, "I am faithful to you." Yet he still asks Him to teach him the way and to help him walk in truth (v. 11). Never stagnant, the God-seeker keeps moving forward in faith.

WHERE ARE WE GOING SO FAST?

Read: Psalm 90:1-12

We fly away. —PSALM 90:10
My days are swifter than a weaver's shuttle. —JOB 7:6

Scientific measurements indicate that we are moving even when we are standing still. Continental landmasses sit on enormous slabs of rock that slide very slowly at the rate of one to eight inches per year. America is gradually moving westward, away from Europe, at the rate of three inches per year.

If that doesn't blow your hair back, consider this. Our Milky Way galaxy is hurtling through space at 375 miles per second or 1.3 million miles per hour. But that's not all. Within our own galaxy the sun and its solar system are zooming along at 12.4 miles per second (43,000 mph) in the direction of the star Vega in the constellation Lyra.

A man lying on his back in a quiet park on a cloudless day may feel as though all time and movement have stopped under the hot rays of a noonday sun. But the scientist and the godly person know otherwise. Just as we are hurtling through the heavens at unimaginable speeds, so too we are moving from here to eternity. Our days and opportunities to live for the Lord pass so rapidly that we cannot afford to waste time.

Teach us to number our days, Lord. Help us to live without desperation or futility as we travel so quickly from our home to yours.

—*Mart DeHaan*

Spending much time on Psalm 90:10 could be a bit of a downer. The verse reminds us of life's brevity—and the fact that there's a general timetable for us all. But as verse 12 tells us, our short time on this planet has as a goal to "gain a heart of wisdom."

HOLDING ON FOR LIFE

Read: Psalm 91

*I will say of the LORD, "He is my refuge and my fortress,
my God, in whom I trust."* —PSALM 91:2

Try to remember a time when you were in a frightening situation. It could have been a near miss in your automobile, or maybe it was footsteps behind you as you walked down a dangerous street. Perhaps you were threatened by the bully in the neighborhood. Possibly you had to face an angry employer. What about the time you were asked to speak before an audience? In all those situations, did you long to have someone close by to give you support and encouragement?

I remember taking my family to the beach one summer day when the waves were quite big. My daughter Katie wanted to go swimming, but she was afraid of those huge breakers. Only after she realized that they didn't move me, and that she was secure as long as she held onto me tightly, could she enjoy the water and the splashing of those waves. She had someone she could depend on for support.

Psalm 91 describes many frightening situations in which we need the assistance of someone stronger than we are. The psalmist tells us that when troubles assailed him from all angles, he went to One who was as strong and unmovable as a fortress. He clung to God for his very survival, for he had learned that when troubles created waves in his life, he could find security and help in Him.

Are you encountering frightening and unnerving situations? Cling to your refuge and fortress, the almighty God. He's the only one to hold onto—for life.

—*Kurt DeHaan*

We all want safety, and this is exactly
what the psalmist offers in Psalm 91:2.
Because God is our refuge and our
fortress, we have the confidence
that no matter what happens,
we have a place of safety.

X

FRESH FRUIT

Read: Psalm 92

The righteous . . . will still bear fruit in old age. —PSALM 92:12, 14

I love the old photographs that are often printed on the obituary page of our local newspaper. A grinning young man in a military uniform and words such as: 92 years old, fought for his country in WWII. Or the young woman with sparkling eyes: 89 years young, grew up on a farm in Kansas during the Depression. The unspoken message is: "I wasn't always old, you know."

Too often, those who have had a long life feel sidelined when they reach their later years. Psalm 92, however, reminds us that no matter how old we are, we can have a fresh and fruitful life. Men and women who have been "planted" in the rich soil of God's vineyard will continue to "bear fruit" and "stay fresh" (v. 14). Jesus promised that those who "remain in [Him]" will continue to "bear much fruit" (John 15:5).

Yes, muscles may ache and joints may hurt, and life may slow down a bit. But inwardly we can be "renewed day by day" (2 Corinthians 4:16).

I recently saw a beautiful white-haired woman wearing a T-shirt that said: "I'm not 80. I'm 18 with 62 years experience." No matter how old we get, we can still be young at heart—but with the benefit of a well-lived lifetime of knowledge and wisdom.

—*Cindy Hess Kasper*

This passage seems to say that we can be useful no matter our age. Like a tree that still draws life from the soil, an older Christian still abiding in the Lord may have the resources to keep active for Him.

MIGHTIER THAN ALL

Read: Psalm 93

The Lord reigns, he is robed in majesty; the Lord is robed in majesty and armed with strength. —PSALM 93:1

Iguazu Falls on the border of Brazil and Argentina is a spectacular waterfall system of 275 falls along 2.7 km (1.67 miles) of the Iguazu River. Etched on a wall on the Brazilian side of the falls are the words of Psalm 93:4, "Mightier than the thunders of many waters, mightier than the waves of the sea, the Lord on high is mighty!" (RSV). Below it are these words, "God is always greater than all of our troubles."

The writer of Psalm 93, who penned its words during the time that kings reigned, knew that God is the ultimate King over all. "The Lord reigns," he wrote. "Your throne was established long ago; you are from all eternity" (vv. 1–2). No matter how high the floods or waves, the Lord remains greater than them all.

The roar of a waterfall is truly majestic, but it is quite a different matter to be in the water hurtling toward the falls. That may be the situation you are in today. Physical, financial, or relational problems loom ever larger and you feel like you are about to go over the falls. In such situations, the Christian has someone to turn to. He is the Lord, "who is able to do immeasurably more than all that we ask or imagine" (Ephesians 3:20) for He is greater than all of our troubles.

—*C. P. Hia*

Interestingly, the psalmist in verse 1 describes God's raiment, not His characteristics. Yet His kingly clothing clearly denotes God's majesty and strength. Perhaps it would have been too much to try to describe God himself.

SUSTAINED IN THE SILENCE

Read: Psalm 94:16-23

In the multitude of my anxieties within me, Your comforts delight my soul.
—PSALM 94:19 (NKJV)

Hudson Taylor (1832–1905) was the founder of the China Inland Mission and a great servant of God. But after the ferocious Boxer Rebellion of 1900, in which hundreds of his fellow missionaries were killed, Taylor was emotionally devastated and his health began to fail. Nearing the end of life's journey, he wrote, "I am so weak that I cannot work. I cannot read my Bible; I cannot even pray. I can only lie still in God's arms like a child and trust."

Have you been passing through a time when you are tired of body and sick of heart? Do you find it difficult to focus your mind on biblical promises? Has it become hard for you to pray? Don't write yourself off as a spiritual castaway. You are joining a host of God's people who have experienced the dark night of the soul.

When we endure such times, all we can do—indeed, all we need do—is lie still like a child in the arms of our heavenly Father. Words aren't necessary. A comforting father doesn't expect his child to make speeches. Neither does God. He knows we need His soothing care. In times of trouble, His mercy holds us up (Psalm 94:18). We may trust Him to carry us through that dark night of the soul and on into the dawning light.

—*Vernon Grounds*

———

Some have translated *delight* in Psalm 94:19 to read "soothe." That's a great picture when combined with the psalmist's "anxieties." We need God's soothing, which can turn an anxious situation into a delight.

THE TRUE OWNER

Read: Psalm 95:1-7

Come, let us bow down in worship, let us kneel before the LORD our Maker; for he is our God. —PSALM 95:6–7

Did you hear about the church that didn't have enough room for parking? Fortunately, it was located right next to a store that was closed on Sundays, so a church member asked the store owner if they could overflow into his parking lot. "No problem," he said. "You can use it 51 weeks out of the year. On the 52nd week, though, it will be chained off." The man was grateful, but asked curiously, "What happens that week?" The storeowner smiled, "Nothing. I just want you to remember that it's not your parking lot."

It's easy to take for granted all the material and spiritual blessings that God has given us. That's why we need to stop and remember that Scripture says the true owner of all we possess is God: "Everything in heaven and earth is yours. Yours, LORD, is the kingdom; you are exalted as head over all" (1 Chronicles 29:11). Even our bodies do not belong to us: "Do you not know that your bodies are temples of the Holy Spirit . . . ? You are not your own; you were bought at a price" (1 Corinthians 6:19–20).

As 1 Timothy 6:17 reminds us: "God . . . richly provides us with everything for our enjoyment." We are so abundantly blessed with good things! Let's never take our Father for granted, but use wisely and gratefully all that He has given us.

—*Cindy Hess Kasper*

———

In Psalm 95:6, the writer makes three references to a position of humility before God: "bow down," "kneel," and "worship." Clearly, we must come before God with this attitude.

SING AGAIN

Read: Psalm 96

Sing to the LORD a new song; sing to the LORD, all the earth.
Sing to the LORD, praise his name. —PSALM 96:1–2

As part of a campaign called "Get America Singing . . . Again," a group of music educators published a list of 42 songs that it feels Americans must continue singing to preserve an important part of the national culture. The list began alphabetically with "Amazing Grace" and ends with "Zip-A-Dee-Doo-Dah." The group's president said, "We have a whole generation that has grown up without singing songs like these—songs that are . . . part of who we are."

Not only in the United States, but also in every country and culture, music is an important part of who people are.

As Christians, we have a wonderful heritage of music. I enjoy using a hymnbook along with the Bible during my time of daily reading and prayer. Sometimes words written many years ago bring a fresh message of hope. I may encounter a familiar song that sparks a memory of God's faithfulness or rekindles a flame of devotion. More than a memory of the past, it becomes a vehicle to praise God today.

Psalm 96:2 encourages us to "sing to the LORD, praise his name; proclaim his salvation day after day." Why not open that long-neglected hymnbook today, rediscover some marvelous messages of faith, and sing . . . again!

—David McCasland

When you sing a favorite song, doesn't each time seem like you are singing it in a fresh and new way? That's the idea of Psalm 96:1. It's really not a new idea—it's a new recounting of the one great story!

X

JUST BECAUSE HE'S GOOD

Read: Psalm 100

*The LORD is good and his love endures forever; his faithfulness
continues through all generations.* —PSALM 100:5

Joel and Lauren decided to move from Washington State back home to Michigan. Wanting to make one last special memory, they bought coffee from their favorite cafe and then stopped at their favorite bookstore. There they picked up two bumper stickers with a favorite motto of the town they were saying goodbye to: "It's an Edmonds kind of day."

After two weeks and a 3,000-mile drive, they entered Michigan. Hungry and wanting to celebrate their arrival, they stopped and asked about where to find a restaurant. Although they had to backtrack a few miles, they found a quaint little cafe. Emma, their waitress, excited to learn they were from her home state of Washington, asked, "What city?" "Edmonds," they replied. "That's where I'm from!" she said. Wanting to share the joy, Joel got their extra bumper sticker from the car and handed it to her. Amazingly, the sticker was from her mother's store! It had gone from her mom's hands to theirs, across 3,000 miles, to her hands.

Mere coincidence? Or were these experiences good gifts orchestrated by a good God who loves to encourage His children? Proverbs tells us, "A person's steps are directed by the LORD" (20:24). In response, let's "praise his name. For the LORD is good" (Psalm 100:4–5).

—Anne Cetas

There's an important theology lesson in Psalm 100:5: God is good, God is eternally merciful, and God's truth endures forever. That's quite a lesson!

INTEGRITY 101

Read: Psalm 101

I will be careful to lead a blameless life . . . . I will conduct the affairs of my house with a blameless heart. —PSALM 101:2

Officials in Philadelphia were astonished to receive a letter and payment from a motorist who had been given a speeding ticket in 1954. John Gedge, an English tourist, had been visiting the City of Brotherly Love when he was cited for speeding. The penalty was $15, but Gedge forgot about the ticket for almost 52 years until he discovered it in an old coat. "I thought, I've got to pay it," said Gedge, 84, who lived in a nursing home in East Sussex when he decided to pay up. "Englishmen pay their debts. My conscience is clear."

This story reminded me of the psalmist David's commitment to integrity. Although he made some terrible choices in his life, Psalm 101 declares his resolve to live blamelessly. His integrity would begin in the privacy of his own house (v. 2) and extend to his choice of colleagues and friends (vv. 6–7). In sharp contrast to the corrupt lives of most kings of the ancient Near East, David's integrity led him to respect the life of his sworn enemy, King Saul (1 Samuel 24:4–6; 26:8–9).

As followers of Jesus, we are called to walk in integrity and to maintain a clear conscience. When we honor our commitments to God and to others, we will walk in fellowship with God. Our integrity will guide us (Proverbs 11:3) and help us walk securely (10:9).

—*Marvin Williams*

As David writes—and as he found out to his own undoing—it is at home where the heart should shine the brightest in its straightforwardness. It's hard to miss the irony of David's words in verse 2.

FIVE-MINUTE RULE

Read: Psalm 102

He will respond to the prayer of the destitute; he will not despise their plea.
—PSALM 102:17

I read about a five-minute rule that a mother had for her children. They had to be ready for school and gather together five minutes before it was time to leave each day.

They would gather around Mom, and she would pray for each one by name, asking for the Lord's blessing on their day. Then she'd give them a kiss and off they'd run. Even neighborhood kids would be included in the prayer circle if they happened to stop by. One of the children said many years later that she learned from this experience how crucial prayer is to her day.

The writer of Psalm 102 knew the importance of prayer. This psalm is labeled, "A prayer of an afflicted person who has grown weak and pours out a lament before the LORD." He cried out, "Hear my prayer, LORD; . . . when I call, answer me quickly" (vv. 1–2). God looks down "from his sanctuary on high, from heaven he view[s] the earth" (v. 19).

God cares for you and wants to hear from you. Whether you follow the five-minute rule asking for blessings on the day, or need to spend more time crying out to Him in deep distress, talk to the Lord each day. Your example may have a big impact on your family or someone close to you.

—*Anne Cetas*

———

The psalmist, while decrying the state of things in Zion, knows that God can restore. He can even restore the "destitute" (v. 17). Ever been there? If so, this verse is for you.

GOD'S HELPERS

Read: Psalm 103:19-22

Praise the LORD, you his angels. —PSALM 103:20

I was having a conversation with some children about God and superheroes when Tobias asked a question. An imaginative, curious five-year-old, he asked anyone listening: "Does God have a sidekick like Hercules does?" His wiser, older brother, age seven, quickly responded: "Yes, He has thousands of them—they're His angels."

Angels are a popular topic of discussion, and people believe a number of myths about them. For instance, some people pray to angels, thinking they are on the same level as God himself. And some believe that people become angels when they die. But here's what the Bible, our authority, teaches:

- God created angels (Colossians 1:15–17).
- Angels worship God (Nehemiah 9:6) and are known by these terms: archangels (Jude 1:9), cherubim (2 Kings 19:15), and seraphim (Isaiah 6:1–3).
- They minister to God's people (Hebrews 1:13–14) by guarding and protecting them (Psalm 91:9–12).
- They are given special assignments by God (Matthew 1:20; Luke 1:26).
- God's angels rejoice when we repent of sin and turn to Christ for salvation (Luke 15:7, 10).

Only God deserves our worship. So let's join the angels in singing His praises!

—Anne Cetas

Here's different admonition to praise God. If God's heavenly hosts—His angels—are called to bless God, then shouldn't we do the same?

THE UNIVERSE IS GOD'S

Read: Psalm 104:31-35

[The LORD] touches the mountains, and they smoke.
—PSALM 104:32

Rising 6.3 miles from its base on the ocean floor and stretching seventy-five miles across, Hawaii's Mauna Loa is the largest volcano on Earth. But on the surface of the planet Mars stands Olympus Mons, the largest volcano yet discovered in our solar system. The altitude of Olympus Mons is three times higher than Mt. Everest and a hundred times more massive than Mauna Loa. It's large enough to contain the entire chain of the Hawaiian Islands!

Long ago, David looked up at the night skies and stood in awe at the wonder of his Creator's universe. He wrote, "The heavens declare the glory of God; the skies proclaim the work of his hands" (Psalm 19:1).

But the stars and the sky were not all that stirred the wonder of ancient writers. Earthquakes and volcanoes also inspired awe for the Creator. Psalm 104 describes God as "he who looks at the earth, and it trembles, who touches the mountains, and they smoke" (v. 32).

As space probes explore more of our solar system, they will continue to discover unknown wonders. But whatever they find is the work of the same Creator (Genesis 1:1).

The wonders of the universe should move us to praise God, just as they moved a shepherd boy long ago as he gazed up at the heavens (Psalm 8:3–5).

—*Dennis Fisher*

While we normally associate such phenomena as volcanoes with the natural reaction of the elements inside the mountain, Psalm 104:32 seems to indicate that God's hand is a part of these events as well.

※

RESCUE AND RESPONSE

Read: Psalm 107:1-9

Let the redeemed of the LORD tell their story—those he redeemed from the hand of the foe. —PSALM 107:2

The sign outside Dave James's shop in Seattle, Washington, says more about getting your life repaired than it does about fixing your vacuum cleaner, but Dave is in business to do both. The top line of the sign is always the same: Free Bibles Inside. The second line changes and features thoughts such as: Surrender Your Heart for a Brand-New Start.

Over the past decade, Mr. James has repaired thousands of vacuum cleaners and given away thousands of Bibles to his customers. It's his way of saying thanks to the Lord for saving him from destruction.

As a successful businessman, Dave James had slipped into a life of drug addiction. "If God hadn't taken cocaine away from me," he says, "I'd be dead." The Lord helped him get clean and find a new beginning.

Every testimony for Christ begins with a rescue followed by a thankful response: "Give thanks to the LORD, for he is good; his love endures forever" (Psalm 107:1).

Whether our experience of salvation sounds dramatic or not, the reality remains: "He has rescued us from the dominion of darkness and brought us into the kingdom of the Son he loves" (Colossians 1:13). Because we have been redeemed, we should want to tell others.

—*David McCasland*

In Psalm 107:2 we read the word *redeemed* one way; the folks to whom it was originally written saw something else. They were redeemed out of Egypt and given a Promised Land east of the Jordan. We've been redeemed from sin and given a Promised Land in heaven. And we need to "tell [our] story."

84

HOW TO ANSWER ACCUSERS

Read: Psalm 109:1-5, 26-31

They accuse me, but I am a man of prayer. —PSALM 109:4

While I was a student at college, my roommate accused me of stealing $100 from him. He didn't confront me directly, but spread his lie among his friends and reported it to the dean's office. The incident was thoroughly investigated, as it should have been.

It was the most helpless experience I have ever faced. All I could do was say, "I didn't do it." But those words seemed hollow against the accusation and rumor.

I didn't know what to do. Part of me wanted to knock the truth out of my roommate. Another part wanted to contact all who heard about it and tell them I was innocent. Only later did my accuser admit that he had faked the theft to get money out of his parents for a stereo.

King David had a similar experience. Someone was making terrible accusations against him, undermining his position and causing him much grief (Psalm 109:2–4).

So what did David do? Did he use his authority to have his accuser killed? No, he prayed and asked the Lord to intercede, punish the slanderer, and make it right (vv. 4–29).

When someone spreads false rumors about us, we may want to retaliate. How much better it is to answer our accusers with the power of prayer!

—*David Egner*

In this psalm, David is facing deceitful and slanderous liars. His response? In the Hebrew the best translation is simply, "But I pray." Can we say that in similar circumstances?

HE LIGHTS THE WAY

Read: Psalm 112

Even in darkness light dawns for the upright, for those who are gracious and compassionate and righteous. —PSALM 112:4

A missionary in Peru told of going one evening to visit a small group of believers. She knew that the house where they were meeting was located on a cliff and that climbing up the pathway would be treacherous. From her own house she took a taxi as far as it could go, and then she began the hazardous ascent to the house. The night was dark and the way was very difficult. As she rounded a bend she suddenly came upon several believers carrying bright lanterns. They had come out to light the way. Her fears relieved, the missionary ascended the path easily and had a good meeting.

In a similar way, God lights our pathway. When we accepted Jesus as our personal Savior, He who is the Light of the World entered our lives and removed the darkness of our sin and despair. This light continues to comfort us through times of sorrow. In the midst of sadness, trouble, illness or disappointment, the Lord brightens the way and encourages His children by giving hope. This may come through a word of exhortation from a fellow believer. It may be the soothing illumination of His Word by the ministry of the Holy Spirit. It may be calm reassurance in response to heartfelt prayer. Or it may be the miraculous supply of a specific need. Whatever the case, God sends light when we are engulfed in darkness of the "valley of the shadow of death."

For the believer, there is always light in the darkest night!

—*David Egner*

Many Christians in days past received hope from this line: "Even in darkness light dawns for the upright."

I LOVE YOU, DADDY

Read: Psalm 116

I love the LORD, for he heard my voice; he heard my cry for mercy.
—PSALM 116:1

Sincere and voluntary expressions of love make for close personal relationships. Nowhere is this more important than in our walk with God. It's one thing to go through the motions of obeying Him out of duty, but it's quite another to serve Him out of a genuine devotion and to tell Him often that we love Him.

The value of voicing our affection was emphasized to me by something my two-year-old daughter did. Although Katie had learned the mechanics of saying, "I love you" by mimicking Mom and Dad as we spoke to her, recently her words took on special meaning. One evening while we were playing together, she ran to me without prompting, put her little arms tightly around my neck and said, "I love you, Daddy!" That moment will always be precious to me. Her words went straight to my heart because they were sincere, unrehearsed, and pure.

Reflecting on that incident, I'm reminded that the Lord desires the same kind of response from each of His spiritual children. As we contemplate what God does for us, we will begin to love and appreciate Him more and more. He gives us new life. He showers us with His favor. He disciplines us in love. He provides us with spiritual gifts to serve Him. And He's building an eternal home for us. When we realize that all these blessings are an expression of His love, we will be eager to show our own love for Him. Then we'll be ready to say, "Jesus, I love you!" Has He heard you tell Him that recently?

—*Kurt DeHaan*

In verses 1–2, we get a great word picture. God leans over and puts His head near us so we can speak into His ear. What a warm picture of God's care for His child!

IN BRIEF

Read: Psalm 117

Great is his love toward us. —PSALM 117:2

I counted once and discovered that Abraham Lincoln's Gettysburg Address contains fewer than three hundred words. This means, among other things, that words don't have to be many to be memorable.

That's one reason I like Psalm 117. Brevity is its hallmark. The psalmist said all he had to say in under thirty words (actually just seventeen words in the Hebrew text).

"Praise the LORD, all you nations; extol him, all you peoples. For great is his love toward us, and the faithfulness of the LORD endures forever. Praise the LORD!"

Ah, that's the good news! Contained in this hallelujah psalm is a message to all nations of the world that God's covenant love "toward us" is "great" (v. 2).

Think about what God's love means. God loved us before we were born; He will love us after we die. Not one thing can separate us from the love of God that is in Jesus our Lord (Romans 8:39). His heart is an inexhaustible and irrepressible fountain of love!

As I read this brief psalm of praise to God, I can think of no greater encouragement for our journey than its reminder of God's merciful kindness. Praise the Lord!

—*David Roper*

Did you know that Paul quoted verse 1 in Romans 15:11? The psalmist, while writing to the Hebrew nation, was given a view of the faith that would include Gentiles as well, as Paul noted.

Ж

A BAD DAY?

Read: Psalm 118:15-24

The Lord has done it this very day; let us rejoice today and be glad.
—PSALM 118:24

Dr. Cliff Arnall, a British psychologist, has developed a formula to determine the worst day of the year. One factor is the time elapsed since Christmas, when the holiday glow has given way to the reality of credit-card bills. Gloomy winter weather, short days, and the failure to keep New Year's resolutions are also a part of Dr. Arnall's calculations. One year, January 24 received the dubious distinction of being "the most depressing day of the year." It usually falls around that time.

Christians are not immune to the effects of weather and post-holiday letdown, but we do have a resource that can change our approach to any day. Psalm 118 recounts a list of difficulties including personal distress (v. 5), national insecurity (v. 10), and spiritual discipline (v. 18), yet it goes on to declare, "This is the day the Lord has made; we will rejoice and be glad in it" (v. 24 NKJV).

The psalm is filled with a celebration of God's goodness and mercy in the midst of trouble and pain. Verse 14 comes as a shout of triumph: "The Lord is my strength and my defense; he has become my salvation."

Even when circumstances hang a sign on our calendar saying "Bad Day!" the Creator enables us to thank Him for the gift of life and to receive each day with joy.

—*David McCasland*

No wonder verse 24 is so encouraging. It is connected to verse 22, which looks ahead to our Savior's coming—"the cornerstone." The "day" in question was probably one of the Old Testament feast days.

FOLLOW THE SIGNAL

Read: Psalm 119:1-8

Oh, that my ways were steadfast in obeying your decrees!
—PSALM 119:5

A driver who ignores traffic signals is "an accident looking for a place to happen." Anyone cheating on red or stopping absentmindedly on green is a danger to himself and to others. Although a series of red lights can be a pain when you're eager to get to your destination, an accident can bring even greater pain.

Several years ago I was happily surprised when a traffic signal was finally installed on a corner that had been especially frustrating to me. It turned a daily ordeal into an orderly and predictable way of getting onto a busy street. Waiting occasionally at a red light is now a pleasure—at least at that intersection of bad memories.

The Scriptures too have some "red lights" that should control our lives as Christians. They are the prohibitions against envy, pride, hatred, irreverence, lust, and selfishness. When the Holy Spirit alerts us to their presence, we should immediately hit the brakes. Likewise, as we move into the heavy traffic of daily living, we must quickly respond by obeying the "green" signals of kindness, humility, love, worship, and purity.

God's stops and starts are designed to help us. We should be as fearful of ignoring a command of Scripture as we are of running a red light.

—*Mart DeHaan*

———

Psalm 119 starts with obedience. We are to "walk according to the law of the LORD" (v. 1), "keep his statutes" (v. 2), and "do no wrong" (v. 3). The goal? To keep God's "decrees."

FROM HEART TO HEART

Read: Psalm 119:9-16

I have hidden your word in my heart that I might not sin against you.
—PSALM 119:11

My childhood piano teacher was a stickler for memorization. Being able to play a piece without error was not enough. I had to play several pieces flawlessly by memory. Her reasoning was this: She didn't want her students to say, when asked to play, "I'm sorry, I don't have my music with me."

As a child, I also memorized Bible passages, including Psalm 119:11. Due to my limited understanding, I believed that simple memorization would keep me from sin. I worked hard at memorizing verses, and I even won a copy of *The Moody Bible Story Book* as an award.

Although memorizing the Bible is a good habit to develop, it's not the act of memorizing that keeps us from sin. As I learned soon after my winning efforts, having the words of Scripture in my head made little difference in my behavior. In fact, instead of victory over sin, knowledge alone generated feelings of guilt.

Eventually I realized that the Word of God had to spread through my whole being. I needed to internalize Scripture, to hide it "in my heart" the way a musician does a piece of music. I had to live the Bible as well as I could quote it. As God's Word spreads from our heads to our hearts, sin loses its power over us.

—*Julie Ackerman Link*

Beginning in verse 9, young people are in focus. They are told to cleanse their ways through the Word. And in verse 11, a specific task is presented: memorizing Scripture. That too helps young people (and old) to avoid sin.

"I DARE YOU!"

Read: Psalm 119:41-48

Never take your word of truth from my mouth, for I have put my hope in your laws. I will always obey your law. —PSALM 119:43-44

I heard a story of a little church that was having a reunion. A former member who attended the celebration had worked hard and had become a millionaire. When he testified about how he had grown in the faith, he related an incident from his childhood.

He said that when he earned his first dollar as a boy, he decided to keep it for the rest of his life. But then a guest missionary preached about the urgent need on the mission fields. He struggled about giving his dollar. "However, the Lord won," the man said proudly, "and I put my treasured dollar in the offering basket. And I am convinced that the reason God has blessed me so much is that when I was a little boy I gave Him everything I possessed." The congregation was awestruck by the testimony—until a little old lady in front piped up, "I dare you to do it again!"

There's a vital truth behind that story. We must not let past attainments stop our spiritual growth. The psalmist said, "I will always obey your law, for ever and ever." He knew he needed to keep his commitment fresh every day.

As Christians, we cannot rest on past attainments. We must give the Lord our full devotion now. Then no one will be able to say to us, "I dare you to do it again!"

—*David Egner*

Living by the Book is an ongoing, everyday thing. To keep God's law continually allows us the special privilege, verse 45 says, of walking "in freedom," unencumbered by the problems that sin introduces into our lives.

THE FORGOTTEN BOOK

Read: Psalm 119:89-104

I delight in your decrees; I will not neglect your word. —PSALM 119:16

A young boy noticed a large black book all covered with dust lying on a high shelf. His curiosity was aroused, so he asked his mother about it. Embarrassed, she hastily explained, "That's a Bible. It's God's Book." The boy thought for a moment and then said, "Well, if that's God's Book, why don't we give it back to Him? Nobody around here uses it anyway."

In many homes, the Bible is hardly used or even thought about. The only time anyone picks it up to read it is when there's trouble, sickness, or a death in the family. And even then, the person may not know where to look for the help that's needed.

How long has it been since you've picked up your Bible and studied it for your own enjoyment, edification, and spiritual growth? Yes, it's God's Book—but He doesn't want it back. He wants you to keep it, to ponder it, to understand it, to believe it, and to obey its message.

That's the primary reason for the devotional guide *Our Daily Bread,* which Our Daily Bread Ministries has produced since 1956. Each devotional article is intended to help you understand God's Word.

Did you read today's Scripture passage? If not, why not do so right now? Don't let the Bible become the forgotten Book in your home.

—Richard DeHaan

How do we delight in decrees?
Isn't that like getting excited about laws?
It's a delight only if we find that
living God's way of righteousness is
better than living man's way of sin.

𝄪

THE CHEAT TEST

Read: Psalm 119:129–136

Direct my footsteps according to your word; let no sin rule over me.
—PSALM 119:133

Dan Ariely, an economics professor at the Massachusetts Institute of Technology, conducted some tests on human behavior. In one experiment, the participants took an examination in which they would receive money for each correct answer. The participants didn't know, however, that Ariely was not testing their knowledge but whether they would cheat. He set up the test so that the groups thought it would be easy to get away with cheating.

Prior to taking the exam, one group was asked to write down as many of the Ten Commandments as they could remember. To Ariely's astonishment, none from this group cheated! But all the other groups did have those who cheated. Recalling a moral benchmark made the difference.

Centuries ago, the psalmist understood the need for a moral benchmark and asked for divine aid in following it. He prayed to the Lord, "Direct my footsteps according to your word; let no sin rule over me. . . . Teach me your decrees" (Psalm 119:133–135).

Ariely's "cheat test" experiment illustrates our need for moral guidance. The Lord has given us His Word as a lamp for our feet and a light for our path (v. 105) to direct us in our moral choices.

—*Dennis Fisher*

———

Verse 134 tells us that letting "sin rule over" us leads to "oppression." Choosing, instead, to get direction from God's Word leads to light (v. 130).

A FAIR TRADE

Read: Psalm 119:161–168

I rejoice in your promise like one who finds great spoil.
—PSALM 119:162

Scott and Mary Crickmore poured 15 years of their lives into helping to translate the New Testament in the Maasina dialect. It was for the Fulani tribe in the West African nation of Mali.

After the initial draft, Mary visited nearby villages and read it to people. She sat in huts with a group of men or women listening to them discuss what they understood. That helped her to make sure the words they were using in the translation were accurate and clear.

Some people would think that the Crickmores' sacrifice was too great—giving up their comfortable lifestyle, changing their diet to mush and rice, and living in less-than-ideal circumstances for those 15 years. But the Crickmores say it was "a fair trade," because now the Fulani people have the Word of God in a language they can read.

The psalmist delighted in God's Word. He stood in awe of it, rejoiced over it, loved it, and obeyed it (Psalm 119:161–168). He found great peace and hope in the Word.

The Fulani people are now able to discover the great treasure (v. 162) of God's Word. Would you agree with the Crickmores that any effort and sacrifice to get the Bible to others is "a fair trade"?

—*Anne Cetas*

———

For a picture of the excitement of discovering God's Word, read 2 Kings 22:3–10. When the Book of the Law was discovered and read to the people, the kingdom of Judah was transformed.

BEYOND THE SHADOWS

Read: Psalm 121

I lift up my eyes to the mountains—where does my help come from?
—PSALM 121:1–2

I love the view of the Rockies from Denver. In the foreground are the foothills, and behind them are the high mountains. On a clear day, one can see Long's Peak, Mount Evans, and other peaks reaching altitudes of 14,000 feet, their tops covered with snow.

Early one morning, as I looked west to the mountains, I saw a sight that filled me with wonder. Because of a layer of low, gray clouds, the foothills lay in heavy shadows. Snow was probably falling. The foothills were dark and ominous, enough to discourage any potential traveler. But beyond them, the white, snow-capped peaks of the high mountains were glistening in the bright sunlight. They seemed to say, "Once you get through the shadows, you'll be all right."

As I looked at that sight, I thought how much it is like our spiritual journey. Ahead we may be able to see only the foothill shadows of hardship, illness, disappointment, and trouble. The way appears foreboding and difficult. But then we lift our eyes higher. There, gleaming afar in the sunlight, are the glorious mountain peaks of God's promises.

Where are you right now? In gloomy foothills, clouded in darkness? Don't despair. Keep moving upward. Sunlit mountain peaks lie just beyond.

—*David Egner*

This is one of the songs of ascent—songs of pilgrims "going up" to Jerusalem to worship. They look up at the mountains—mountains that at times held pagan shrines ("high places" of the kingdom era)—and ask where their help originates. The answer in verse 2 is "from the LORD."

HE NEVER SLEEPS

Read: Psalm 121

He will not let your foot slip—he who watches over you will not slumber.
—PSALM 121:3

Giraffes have the shortest sleep cycle of any mammal. They sleep only between 10 minutes and 2 hours in a 24-hour period and average just 1.9 hours of sleep per day. Seemingly always awake, the giraffe has nothing much in common with most humans in that regard. If we had so little sleep, it would probably mean we had some form of insomnia. But for giraffes, it's not a sleep disorder that keeps them awake. It's just the way God has made them.

If you think 1.9 hours a day is not much sleep, consider this fact about the Creator of our tall animal friends: Our heavenly Father *never* sleeps.

Describing God's continual concern for us, the psalmist declares, "He who watches over you will not slumber" (Psalm 121:3). In the context of this psalm, the writer makes it clear that God's sleepless vigilance is for our good. Verse 5 says, "The LORD watches over you." God protects us and cares for us—with no need for refreshing. Our Protector is constantly seeking our good. As one song puts it: "He never sleeps, He never slumbers. He watches me both night and day."

Are you facing difficulties? Turn to the One who never sleeps. Each second of each day, let Him "watch over your coming and going" (v. 8).

—*Bill Crowder*

———

Throughout Israel's history, the people often worshiped pagan gods. These entities had human characteristics. For instance, they slept. It was important then for the people to be reminded that God will "neither slumber nor sleep" (121:4) as they traveled treacherous paths.

DYING IN THE SERVICE

Read: Psalm 122

I rejoiced with those who said to me, "Let us go to the house of the LORD."
—PSALM 122:1

As a little boy was sitting in church, his eyes were attracted to a large flag bearing a number of gold stars. Turning to his father, he whispered, "Daddy, why does that flag have all those stars on it?" "To remind us of those who died in the service," was the reply. A puzzled look came over the boy's face. After thinking for a few moments about what his father said, he asked with childish innocence, "Daddy, did they die in the morning or evening service?"

We smile, yet the lad's misunderstanding suggests a sobering fact—many do "die in the service" every Sunday. I'm thinking about those who are turned off by the order of worship and find everything quite boring. They attend simply because it's the thing to do. As far as any spiritual benefit is concerned, they might just as well be dead.

The psalmist declared, "I rejoiced with those who said to me, 'Let us go to the house of the Lord.' " We know, of course, that when David referred to "the house of the LORD," he had Jerusalem in mind. Nevertheless, we should have the same attitude about going to church. When we enter our place of worship expecting a blessing, we'll receive one. You see, it's up to us. If we are faithful in attending a church where the Word of God is really believed and preached, if we go sincerely desiring the Lord's best, and if we have prayerfully prepared our own hearts, there will be no "dying in the service." Instead, the ministry of the Word, the singing of God's praise, and the fellowship of the Lord's people will bring spiritual health to our needy souls.

—Richard DeHaan

In Psalm 122, the people are nearing their goal—God's temple, where they will worship. There is an excitement in their voices, and we can imagine a spring in their step as they look forward to being with God's people in prayer and sacrifice.

✕

KEEP LAUGHING

Read: Psalm 126

Our mouths were filled with laughter, our tongues with songs of joy.
—PSALM 126:2

A judge has ordered a German man to stop bursting into laughter in the woods. Joachim Bahrenfeld, an accountant, was taken to court by one of several joggers who say their runs have been disturbed by Bahrenfeld's deafening squeals of joy. He faces up to 6 months in jail if he is caught again. Bahrenfeld, 54, says he goes to the woods to laugh nearly every day to relieve stress. "It is part of living for me," he says, "like eating, drinking, and breathing." He feels that a cheerful heart, expressed through hearty laughter, is important to his health and survival.

A merry heart is vital in life. Proverbs 17:22 says, "A cheerful heart is good medicine." A happy heart affects our spirit and our physical health.

But there is a deeper, abiding joy for those who trust the Lord that is based on much more than frivolity and circumstances. It is a joy based on God's salvation. He has provided forgiveness of sin and a restored relationship with himself through His Son Jesus. That gives us a deep joy that circumstances cannot shake (Psalm 126:2–3; Habakkuk 3:17–18; Philippians 4:7).

May you experience the joy of knowing Jesus Christ today!
—*Marvin Williams*

What was all the laughing about in verse 2? Clearly, the people were beside themselves with joy because they had been released from captivity in Babylon and were allowed to return home. The Lord had indeed "done great things for them" (126:2).

WE ALL NEED MERCY

Read: Psalm 130

With the LORD is unfailing love and with him is full redemption.
—PSALM 130:7

I was reminded the other day that all of us need mercy. I read about a lady who stormed into a photography studio with a set of proofs and declared indignantly that they didn't do her justice. Looking her full in the face, the man behind the counter remarked wryly, "Lady, you don't need justice—you need mercy!" But don't we all? I remember many times in my own life when people acted graciously toward me. My parents, my teachers, my wife, my employers, and even the members of my former churches have often overlooked my failures. They've all treated me with loving kindness rather than harsh justice.

If we must have mercy from others, how much more we need it from God! The words of Psalm 130:3 often come to my mind when I am alone with Him: "If you, LORD, kept a record of sins, Lord, who could stand?" How glad I am that He keeps forgiving.

As I write this devotional, I recall vividly the day I answered the telephone to hear a pastor friend on the other end of the line say, "My brother, do you know, 'it is because of the Lord's mercies that we are not consumed'?" Yes, I knew. I relied upon His grace when I received Christ, and His acceptance of me then was just the beginning of the goodness and favor He has been showering upon me ever since.

Have you acknowledged that you owe everything to God? Have you thanked Him for His kindly forbearance in forgiving you again, and again, and again? You should, because we all need mercy!

—*Herb Vander Lugt*

Examine the beauty of this verse: "I wait for the Lord more than watchmen wait for the morning" (130:6). Indeed in God alone there is hope.

RAINED OUT!

Read: Psalm 135:1-7

Praise the Lord. . . . He sends lightning with the rain and brings out the wind from his storehouses. —PSALM 135:1, 7

You have probably heard testimonies of how Christians prayed and the rain stopped just before an outdoor service began. Or perhaps it didn't start pouring until the final "Amen." Nowhere in the Bible, however, does God promise that He will always answer in such a dramatic way.

One autumn I was asked to speak at an outdoor evangelistic service at a county fair in Michigan. It was to begin at 2:30 p.m. The grandstands were full. A fine Christian high school choir was in place. We had prayed for the service, even as heavy, dark clouds were gathering. Then, just as the first hymn was announced, a violent storm swept through the fairgrounds. Swirling winds and driving rain lashed the grandstand. Lightning flashed and thunder roared. It wasn't long until we were forced to cancel the service. We were rained out!

Did this mean that God had lost control of His universe? Absolutely not! Were we out of His will for trying to hold an evangelistic service? No. It simply meant that at 2:30 that afternoon in Centreville, Michigan, God had different plans.

Whether God stops the rain or lets it pour, we can be sure that He is in control and He will do what is best. And we can praise the Lord for that.

—*David Egner*

God's sovereignty, according to verse 7, extends even to the lightning, the rain, and the wind. The psalmist tells us that those things come from God's "storehouses," or treasuries.

A SAFE PAIR OF HANDS

Read: Psalm 138

With your right hand you save me. —PSALM 138:7

Edwin van der Sar, goalkeeper for the Manchester United soccer team, had a "safe" pair of hands. He kept the ball from entering his team's goal for 1,302 minutes, a world record in one season! That means that for almost 15 games of 90 minutes each, no one was able to score even one goal against his team while he was guarding the goalposts. But one goal by an opposing team in March 2009 ended his record.

The psalmist David found comfort in the safest pair of hands—God's hands. He wrote of God's protection in Psalm 138, "You stretch out your hand . . . with your right hand you save me" (v. 7). Like David, we can look to God's safe hands to keep us from spiritual danger and defeat.

Another assurance from God's Word for followers of Christ is Jude 1:24–25: "To him who is able to keep you from stumbling and to present you before his glorious presence without fault and with great joy—to the only God our Savior be glory, majesty, power and authority, through Jesus Christ our Lord, before all ages, now and forevermore! Amen." That doesn't mean we'll never stumble. But it does mean we won't stumble so badly that God cannot pick us up.

God's safe pair of hands can never fail—ever!

—*C. P. Hia*

____

In Psalm 138, we hear the echo of Psalm 136:12. God did not want His people to forget that He had delivered them from captivity in Egypt.

THOSE INNER FLAWS

Read: Psalm 138

The LORD will perfect that which concerns me.
—PSALM 138:8 (NKJV)

Most of us will admit that we have personality flaws and character weaknesses. We see undesirable tendencies in ourselves, such as selfishness, irritability, impatience, cruelty, vindictiveness, hotheadedness. They are with us because of our fallen sinful condition. Yet many Christians testify that their defects and weaknesses have become a blessing, causing them to rely more heavily on Jesus. By acknowledging their weakness, these believers have experienced God's grace and strength.

We can see this link between imperfection and improvement all around us in nature. Take, for instance, the formation of crystals, which make up our valuable minerals and precious stones. Scientists tell us that few things develop more orderly and predictably than crystals. Each kind of mineral and gem has its own special shape or appearance. In addition, every one of them is made up of a great number of atoms stacked in perfect alignment. Occasionally, though, one of these basic particles gets out of line. Surprisingly, these occurrences are essential steps in the development of crystals. They give them their most beautiful properties. Most gems owe their brilliant colors to these flaws.

Have you been worried about faults or shortcomings in your life? Don't let them get you down. Instead, admit their presence, commit them to the Lord in prayer, and trust Him to give you victory. The psalmist said, "The Lord will perfect that which concerns me."

—*Mart DeHaan*

Notice David's reference to trouble in Psalm 138:7 and then the reminder of God's work in his life in verse 8. God accomplishes His work despite our humanity and failures.

COMMUNION ON THE MOON

Read: Psalm 139:1-12

If I go up to the heavens, you are there. —PSALM 139:8

Apollo 11 landed on the surface of the moon on Sunday, July 20, 1969. Most of us are familiar with Armstrong's historic statement as he stepped onto the moon's surface: "That's one small step for a man; one giant leap for mankind." But few know about the first meal eaten there.

Buzz Aldrin had brought aboard the spacecraft a tiny communion kit provided by his church. Aldrin sent a radio broadcast to earth asking listeners to contemplate the events of that day and to give thanks.

Then, in radio blackout for privacy, Aldrin poured wine into a silver chalice. He read, "I am the vine; you are the branches. If you remain in me and I in you, you will bear much fruit" (John 15:5). Silently, he gave thanks and partook of the bread and cup.

God is everywhere, and our worship should reflect this reality. In Psalm 139 we are told that wherever we go, God is intimately present with us. Buzz Aldrin celebrated that experience on the surface of the moon. Thousands of miles from earth, he took time to commune with the One who created, redeemed, and fellowshipped with him.

Are you far from home? Do you feel as if you're on a mountaintop or in a dark valley? No matter what your situation, God's fellowship is only a prayer away.

—Dennis Fisher

Ever try to hide from God? No matter where we go—even to the moon or to the remotest place on earth—God is there, desiring a personal relationship with us.

WONDERFULLY MADE

Read: Psalm 139:13-18

Your works are wonderful, I know that full well. —PSALM 139:14

While getting an eye exam recently, my doctor hauled out a piece of equipment that I hadn't seen before. I asked him what the device was, and he responded, "I'm using it to take a picture of the inside of the back of your eye."

I was impressed that someone had invented a camera that could do that. But I was even more impressed by what my doctor could learn from that picture. He said, "We can gather a lot of details about your current general health simply by looking at the back of your eye."

My doctor's comment amazed me. It is remarkable that a person's overall health can be measured by the health of the eye. What care the Lord has taken to place these details in the bodies He has created! It immediately brings to my mind the words of David, the psalmist, who reveled in God's creativity: "I praise you because I am fearfully and wonderfully made; your works are wonderful, I know that full well" (Psalm 139:14).

The enormous complexities of our bodies reflect the genius and wisdom of our great Creator. The wonder of His design is more than breathtaking—it gives us countless reasons to worship Him!

—*Bill Crowder*

————

Inside every soul are the truth of God's existence and the reality of His marvelous creation. Think for a moment about your body and the multitudes of ways God's creative power is seen in it.

A FRESH GLIMPSE OF GLORY

Read: Psalm 145:1-13

They speak of the glorious splendor of your majesty —and I will meditate on your wonderful works. —PSALM 145:5

Every summer, thousands of *Good Morning America* viewers cast their votes to select "The Most Beautiful Place in America." I was delighted when one year the winner was announced, and it was Sleeping Bear Dunes National Lakeshore in my home state of Michigan. Admittedly, I didn't expect the winning location to be in my own backyard. It reminded me of the time my wife, Martie, and I visited Niagara Falls. A man nearby watched our tourist behavior and quipped, "Ain't nothin' to it. I see it every day."

How easily we grow accustomed to our surroundings and dulled to things that are familiar—even places and experiences that once brought great delight. Although God's glory is clearly displayed all around us, sometimes the busyness of everyday life blocks our view. We take for granted His amazing work in our lives. We lose the wonder of the cross. We forget the privilege of being His child. We neglect the pleasure of His presence and miss the beauty of His creation.

I love the psalmist's declaration: "I will meditate on your wonderful works" (Psalm 145:5). Let's take time today to meditate on God's "wonderful works" and get a fresh glimpse of His glory!

—*Joe Stowell*

———

Literally, the phrase "glorious splendor" can be translated from the Hebrew to be "the glory of the splendor of the majesty." That's a great combination of descriptive words for us to meditate on!

NOT ENOUGH STARS

Read: Psalm 147

Sing to the LORD with grateful praise. —PSALM 147:7

"I like to play with the stars," a little girl told her pastor one day when he came to visit her. She was bedridden due to a severe spinal deformity, and her bed was positioned so that she had a good view of the sky. She wanted it that way so she could see the stars at night. "You see, many nights I wake up and can't get back to sleep," she told the minister, "and it's then that I play with the stars."

Her pastor, curious about what she meant by that, asked, "How do you play with the stars?" The child answered, "I pick out one and say, 'That's Mommy.' I see another and say, 'That's Daddy.' And I just keep on naming the stars after people and things I'm thankful for—my brothers and sisters, my doctor, my friends, my dog." And on and on she went, until at last she exclaimed, "But there just aren't enough stars to go around!"

Do you ever feel that way when you think about the many blessings God has showered on you? Of course, you could never name all your material, physical, spiritual, temporal, and eternal blessings. But from time to time, it's good to remember with gratitude His many favors. As you do, like that little girl, you'll feel like exclaiming, "There just aren't enough stars to go around!"

—*Richard DeHaan*

———

Psalm 146:2 seems to indicate that praising God is a lifetime proposition: "I will sing praise to my God as long as I live." There's so much to praise, it would take that long to do it properly.

HALLELUJAH!

Read: Psalm 148

Let them praise the name of the LORD, for his name alone is exalted.
—PSALM 148:13

Recently I saw a television commercial that made it appear that fish and animals were singing "The Hallelujah Chorus." At first it seemed a bit absurd and even sacrilegious to see angelfish and brown bears mouthing the word *hallelujah*. But as I thought about it, a passage of Scripture came to mind.

Psalm 148 calls for everything in creation to praise the Lord. Included in the invitation are "great sea creatures" (v. 7), "wild animals and all cattle, small creatures and flying birds" (v. 10). Not exactly the usual crowd in the choir loft or the congregation on Sunday morning!

As you read Psalm 148, count the number of different elements of God's creation that are invited to join in praising the Lord. Among them are angels, stars, sea creatures, mountains, trees, animals, kings and princes, men and women, young and old.

The psalmist cried out, "Let them praise the name of the LORD, for his name alone is exalted; his splendor is above the earth and the heavens" (v. 13). Is anyone or anything excluded from this invitation? It appears not.

On this day and throughout the year, may each of us answer this call to praise God in a joyful and lasting way. Let's join all creation in celebrating the greatness of our God!

—*David McCasland*

What does it take to give God adequate praise? Angels. Sun and moon. Stars. Highest heavens. Waters above the skies. Sea creatures. Mountains. Kings and princes. Young men and women. The list goes on. That's what it takes.

A LESSON IN PRAISE

Read: Psalm 150

Praise the Lord. —PSALM 150:1

Psalm 150 is not only a beautiful expression of praise, it's also a lesson in praising the Lord. It tells us where to praise, why we're to praise, how we're to praise, and who should offer praise.

Where do we praise? In God's "sanctuary" and "mighty heavens" (v. 1). Wherever we are in the world is a proper place to praise the One who created all things.

Why do we praise? First, because of what God does. He performs "acts of power." Second, because of who God is. The psalmist praised Him for "his surpassing greatness" (v. 2). The all-powerful Creator is the Sustainer of the universe.

How should we praise? Loudly. Softly. Soothingly. Enthusiastically. Rhythmically. Boldly. Unexpectedly. Fearlessly. In other words, we can praise God in many ways and on many occasions (vv. 3–5).

Who should praise? "Everything that has breath" (v. 6). Young and old. Rich and poor. Weak and strong. Every living creature. God's will is for everyone to whom He gave the breath of life to use that breath to acknowledge His power and greatness.

Praise is our enthusiastic expression of gratitude to God for reigning in glory forever.

—Julie Ackerman Link

Like a song that rises to a crescendo, Psalm 150 ends the Psalms with a glorious musical climax as the instruments strain to glorify God.

OUR DAILY BREAD WRITERS

HENRY BOSCH

The first editor of *Our Daily Bread,* Henry loved to sing—and actually did some recording for Radio Bible Class in its early years.

DAVE BRANON

An editor with Discovery House, Dave has been involved with *Our Daily Bread* since the 1980s. He has written several books, including *Beyond the Valley* and *Stand Firm,* both Discovery House publications.

ANNE CETAS

After becoming a Christian in her late teens, Anne was introduced to *Our Daily Bread* and began reading it right away. Now she reads it for a living as the senior content editor of *Our Daily Bread.*

BILL CROWDER

A former pastor who is now an associate teacher for Our Daily Bread Ministries, Bill travels extensively as a Bible conference teacher, sharing God's truths with believers in Malaysia and Singapore and other places where the ministry has international offices.

DENNIS DEHAAN

When Henry Bosch retired, Dennis became the second managing editor of *Our Daily Bread.* A former pastor, he loved preaching and teaching the Word of God.

KURT DEHAAN

A grandson of Dr. M. R. DeHaan, Kurt was the managing editor of *Our Daily Bread* for several years. He held that position until the late summer of 2003 when he died of a heart attack at age fifty while enjoying his customary lunchtime jog.

MART DEHAAN

The former president of Our Daily Bread Ministries, Mart followed in the footsteps of his grandfather M. R. and his dad, Richard, in that capacity. Mart, who has long been associated with *Day of Discovery* as host of the program from Israel, is now senior content advisor for Our Daily Bread Ministries.

RICHARD DEHAAN

Son of the founder of Our Daily Bread Ministries, Dr. M. R. DeHaan, Richard was responsible for the ministry's entrance into television. Under his leadership, *Day of Discovery*, the ministry's long-running TV program, made its debut in 1968.

DAVID EGNER

A retired Our Daily Bread Ministries editor and longtime *Our Daily Bread* writer, David was also a college professor during his working career. In fact, he was a writing instructor for both Anne Cetas and Julie Ackerman Link at Cornerstone University.

DENNIS FISHER

As a research editor at Our Daily Bread Ministries, Dennis uses his theological training to guarantee biblical accuracy. He is also an expert in C. S. Lewis studies.

VERNON GROUNDS

A longtime college president (Denver Seminary) and board member for Our Daily Bread Ministries, Vernon's life story was told in the Discovery House book *Transformed by Love*.

C. P. HIA

A resident of Singapore, C. P. has been a men's Bible study leader for the past twenty years, and he also volunteers his services in the Our Daily Bread Ministries office in his homeland—the only island city-state in the world. He has written for *Our Daily Bread* since 2008.

CINDY HESS KASPER

An editor for the Our Daily Bread Ministries publication *Our Daily Journey*, Cindy began writing for *Our Daily Bread* in 2006.

JULIE ACKERMAN LINK

A book editor by profession, Julie wrote for *Our Daily Bread* from 2000 to 2015. Her book *Above All, Love* was published in 2008 by Discovery House. Julie passed away on April 10, 2015, after a lengthy battle with cancer.

DAVID MCCASLAND

A resident of Colorado, David enjoys the beauty of God's grandeur as displayed in the Rocky Mountains. An accomplished biographer, David has written several books, including *Oswald Chambers: Abandoned to God* and *Eric Liddell: Pure Gold*.

HADDON ROBINSON

Haddon has taught hundreds of young preachers the art of preaching. He is former president of Denver Seminary and served for many years as a professor at Gordon-Conwell Theological Seminary.

DAVID ROPER

David lives in Idaho, where he takes advantage of the natural beauty of his state. He has been writing for *Our Daily Bread* since 2000, and he has published several successful books with Discovery House.

JENNIFER BENSON SCHULDT

Chicagoan Jennifer Schuldt writes from the perspective of a mom of a growing family. She has written for *Our Daily Bread* since 2010, and she also pens articles for another Our Daily Bread Ministries publication, *Our Daily Journey*.

JOE STOWELL

As president of Cornerstone University, Joe stays connected to today's young adults in a leadership role. A popular speaker and a former pastor, Joe has written a number of books over the years, including *Strength for the Journey* and *Jesus Nation*.

HERB VANDER LUGT

For many years, Herb was the research editor at Our Daily Bread Ministries, responsible for checking the biblical accuracy of the booklets published by the ministry. A World War II veteran, Herb spent several years as a pastor before his Our Daily Bread Ministries tenure began.

PAUL VAN GORDER

A writer for *Our Daily Bread* in the 1980s and 1990s, Paul was a noted pastor and Bible teacher—both in the Atlanta area where he lived and through the *Day of Discovery* TV program.

MARVIN WILLIAMS

Marvin's first foray into Our Daily Bread Ministries came as a writer for *Our Daily Journey*. In 2007, he penned his first *Our Daily Bread* article. Marvin is pastor of a church in Lansing, Michigan.

NOTE TO THE READER

The publisher invites you to share your response to the message of this book by writing Discovery House, P.O. Box 3566, Grand Rapids, MI 49501, U.S.A. For information about other Discovery House books, music, or DVDs, contact us at the same address or call 1-800-653-8333. Find us on the Internet at dhp.org or send an e-mail to books@dhp.org.